100 IDE
FOR TEACHING DRAMA

CONTINUUM ONE HUNDREDS SERIES

100 IDEAS
FOR TEACHING
DRAMA

Johnnie Young

continuum

Continuum International Publishing Group

The Tower Building	80 Maiden Lane
11 York Road	Suite 704
London	New York
SE1 7NX	NY 10038

www.continuumbooks.com

First published 2007
Reprinted 2009, 2010, 2011

British Library Cataloguing-in-Publication Data
A catalogue record for this book is available from the British
Library.

ISBN: 9780826485489 (paperback)

Library of Congress Cataloging-in-Publication Data
Young, Johnnie.
  100 ideas for teaching drama / Johnnie Young.
    p.cm.
  ISBN-13: 978-0-8264-8548-9 (pbk.)
  ISBN-10: 0-8264-8548-0 (pbk.)
  1. Drama in education. 2. Drama—Study and teaching
(Secondary) I. Title.

  PN3171.Y68 2008
  792.071'2—dc22

                                        2007045512

Designed and typeset by Ben Cracknell Studios |
www.benstudios.co.uk
Printed and bound in India

*This book is dedicated to my wife Sylvie
and my children Edward, Julie and William.*

CONTENTS

SECTION 3 **Characters and Lives**

SECTION 4 Exploring the World

SECTION 5 Stage Craft

SECTION 6 **Bringing Language and Literature Alive**

SECTION 7 **Media**

SECTION 8 **Ideas for Mini-Plays**

ACKNOWLEDGEMENTS

I would like to thank my drama teachers who have taught me so much over the years: David Chapman, Chris Young, Franc Chadwick, and at drama school the actor Anthony Carrick.

INTRODUCTION

These 100 original ideas have all been tried and tested with students over the years in various adaptations and versions. With a bit of imagination the ideas can work for all ages and abilities.

I have found that the best way to get the most from your students and to engage and develop interest in drama is to guide them through an example and then encourage them to think up an idea of their own. They need a framework and an example to latch onto in order to fire their imaginations, but once they have been given this, they will produce wonderful results.

In many cases it is good to watch some kind of performance, which after all is the essence of drama and then give feedback that emphasizes the good parts and gently points the way for areas to work on next time. I feel that the vital feedback session should always be led by the teacher, who will sensitively give the comments. The temperature of the feedback must always be one of warm encouragement to experiment and explore further.

In the drama class I have found that the following rules are absolutely vital:

- ○ The teacher is at all times the leader. Sometimes this is much more apparent than at other times, but the instructions, guidance and control must come from the teacher.
- ○ The teacher must have a 'freeze' command and when this is given it is crucial that every member of the group complies.
- ○ The audience must always behave well.
- ○ Safety is very important. In the vast majority of activities, no physical contact is required (or desired) between students.

- If somebody laughs at somebody else's efforts in a way designed to put them down, then that person should forfeit their right to do drama with that group.
- The acting space should always be clean and tidy and uncluttered.
- Routines should be established on how activities are set up, developed and displayed.
- Never force anyone to act in front of others. The best way is to start with volunteers and gently encourage others to join in.

The ideas in this book cover the whole spectrum of drama-type activities. Once an idea is taken up, the philosophy is to expand, develop and experiment.

When set up correctly, presented in the right way, developed and experimented with, performed and praised, the power and magic of a drama lesson is fantastic. It is a question of setting up a situation so that the incredible imaginations of the students can be unleashed.

A final word. Many teachers try, understandably, to relate all the activities to the young person's world. The amazing discovery made by every good drama teacher is that, with the right framework, the students can easily enter into any imaginative world they choose. It is at this point that the students begin to teach the teacher. I hope these ideas help you to have great lessons.

Storytelling

AIM: To practise creating freeze frames; narration; sequencing and structuring of presentations.

Create, or have your students create, three very different freeze frames and pick one student to illustrate each freeze frame. Here is an example of three different characters to be played by students whom we shall refer to as (A), (B) and (C):

(A): Sitting looking depressed and downhearted with his shoulders slumped and his head resting on his chest.

(B): Standing proudly with his chest puffed up in great importance and confidence in the middle of giving instructions to someone.

(C): Just about to sign an autograph in a notebook for a 'fan'.

Arrange the characters around the acting space. A narrator saunters around them explaining their present situations. For example:

"(A) was once very successful and wealthy but a sequence of bad luck led to him losing everything."

"(B) was very disadvantaged earlier in his life but was able to start, build up and run his own business. He is now a multimillionaire!"

"(C) was gifted at sports at school and became a successful and famous sportsperson. But there was a turning point in his life that changed everything."

Two of the key students then leave the acting area, leaving one behind. This student will now act out how he came to be in the initial freeze frame using a series of freeze frames depicting his past. A narrator will explain what is going on in each frame.

Here is an outline of the way this could be done for (A):

Freeze frame 1: (A) is holding open a newspaper and is looking with great interest at the contents. The narrator says, "Years ago he studied the financial pages and became an expert at investing in shares."

Freeze frame 2: (A) is holding a glass of champagne and smiling as he looks out from his yacht across the sea to his tropical island. The narrator says, "He invested well and made more and more money. He also started to spend and spend and spend. He bought yachts and helicopters and islands . . ."

Freeze frame 3: (A) is seated facing his bank manager. The bank manager is looking with dismay at his accounts. The narrator says, "If you spend more than you earn there comes a time when the whole thing collapses! He became bankrupt!"

The freeze frames can be held for the duration of the narration. Guide students to work out similar scenario freeze frames for student (B) and student (C).

At the end, the key characters adopt their original positions but because the audience now knows more about them, their presence has more dramatic interest.

AIM: For students to work collaboratively and develop skills worked on in Idea 1.

In this idea the students are going to act out key moments from their lives while the events are narrated by a partner. Start by dividing the group into pairs and asking them to decide on key moments in their lives. A good way to get them to focus on what they should talk about is to provide them with a worksheet highlighting key events of a famous person's life. This works particularly well if the famous person is someone currently in the news. Try and have a variety of experiences: good, bad and interesting. Once they've decided on the key events, they should prepare a series of silent sequences to illustrate what's happening. Their partner should prepare a narration of the event.

The best way to do this is for the narrator to speak first while the actor is still, and then for the actor to act out the situation (usually slowly and with emphasis) as the speaker looks on quietly. It takes a little practice to get the timing and rhythm to flow.

Here is a worked example:

Narrator: "When I was very small my first memory was reaching for that cup, right up there on that table." (The acting student then acts out reaching for the cup, as if he was a toddler.)

Narrator: "Suddenly, I caught it and I remember waking up in hospital with bandages around my head!" (The student lies on the floor to illustrate.)

Narrator: "Then, when I was about eight, a wonderful piece of luck! I had been walking on the beach for hours, searching its surface for treasure when . . ." (Student acts out finding a really valuable find.)

When they have practised in pairs ask a few to present their work to the class.

AIM: To dramatically interpret a story.

Divide the class into pairs. One student should narrate a made-up story while the other acts it out. The story can be on any topic, however there must be a sequence of clearly linked events. It works better when each part of the story is short. Allow plenty of take-up time for the actor to think and react. The actor doesn't know what is coming next. For example:

Narrator: "She looked around her, a little nervously."
Actor: (looks around)
Narrator: "She decides that she will explore the forest. She starts slowly."
Actor: (slowly walks towards the 'forest' looking intently around. (A good tip, which suggests the illusion of distance, is to walk in a circular direction around the acting space.))
Narrator: "Suddenly she stops! What was that? It seemed to come from up there."
Actor: (stops and looks up slowly, perhaps her body language shows signs of fear)
Narrator: "It was a bird! She sighs and continues her journey, unaware at this stage that some strange thing is following her . . ."

And so on. Once the rhythm and flow is established this works well because students are great natural storytellers. The teacher may wish to observe and comment here and there in order to enhance the storyline and suggest interesting ways of doing things.

EXTENSION IDEA
Try:

One narrator with a small group of actors acting out the story.

One actor and several narrators, each taking it in turns to tell the story and each developing it in their own way.

5

AIM: To use collaborative storytelling and share the creative process through improvisation.

Sit the group down in a large circle and nominate one student to stand in the centre. Ask another student to name a story genre (e.g. horror, thriller, love, war, adventure, ghost, mystery etc.). The rest of the students then have to create a story based on this genre. The student to the left of the first student generates the first line (which should include clear instructions for the actor in the centre of the circle). The next student generates the second line and the story moves around the circle. In response to each instruction, the student standing in the centre of the circle starts to act.

When the story gets back to the first person (who started the narration), that person gets up and the student who has acted sits down. The genre is changed and a new story begins (or the old one continues). For example:

Student 1: "Horror." (the genre)

Student 2: "It is a cold foggy night and Andrew is lost. He stumbles around, holding his hands out and feeling for trees."

Student 3: "Is that a light he sees in the distance?"

Student 4: "He starts to walk slowly towards the light."

Student 5: "Suddenly . . ."

Student 6: "He stops. What was that awful noise?"

Student 7: "It sounded like a howl."

TIPS: It works well when the teacher directs by silently pointing to the next student in turn. If a student doesn't want to say anything, quickly point to the next student to keep the flow going. Likewise, if a student doesn't want to get up and act, move on to the next student swiftly. If there is a lull in the rhythm be ready to quickly fill the gap.

FROM DREAM TO REALITY

AIM: For students to predict future events and present them dramatically.

Ask students to think of something they would love to do or be or own. It may be a dream job or the ability to play a musical instrument or the ownership of a sports car.

The activity is in three parts: first, explaining what their aspirations for the future are, say, in ten years' time. Second, showing with key scene role plays, how they achieved it, and third, showing the dream as reality. For example:

PART 1: THE DREAM

A student says, "In ten years I want to be a vet. I love animals and what could be better than making sick animals well again?"

PART 2: THE KEY SCENES

This part could show brief moments along his road to success by way of little role plays. It might show him asking a local vet if he could help out on Saturdays. Another scene may show him reading his examination mark for biology and cheering! Then the first day at university, perhaps a phone call with mum where he is saying how hard it all is and he wants to chuck it in. Mum encourages him to keep going! Another scene may show him as a vet with his first customer and how nervous he is.

PART 3: EXPLAINING THE REALITY OF THE DREAM

Here the student explains how things are now (ten years on, dream achieved – working as a vet).

HOW DOES IT END?

AIM: To allow students to dramatically create their own ending from a given opening scene.

Create the opening scene of a story and read this to the class. Then divide them into groups of four or five and get them to act out how they think the story will end. For example:

Sarah is a bright outgoing energetic teenager. Against her wishes she is staying for a week's holiday with her Aunt Maud. Aunt Maud is a strict, severe, unforgiving and bitter woman. If things don't go her way she gets very angry. Sarah had been told by her aunt to be careful with two large Chinese vases in the hallway. They are antique and very valuable. Sarah was practising a dance and accidentally kicked one vase into the other. Both vases are smashed into a thousand tiny pieces. In five minutes her aunt will return from shopping . . .

Once you have given the students time to work through their plays, have a couple of groups act out their work for the class. End by discussing how different groups have interpreted the story differently.

AIM: To understand how the use of flashbacks works when illustrating past events.

Students seem to really enjoy pretending to be old people, so divide your class into groups. The idea is for one of the old people to discuss an event in the past and then for the other students to act out this reminiscence. For example:

Three old people are sitting dozing in the lounge of an old people's home. A conversation starts up about the past. One of them says, "I remember when the two gangs met up. There were 1,200 on their side and 600 on ours. Yes, we had a few scuffles but nobody got hurt that day. Everyone went home happy. Yes, I remember it well! Poor old policeman . . . There was only one on duty that day . . . I can still picture his face."

She slowly slumps into a sleep and the past is re-enacted:

Three students represent one group and six students represent the other. The groups move slowly towards each other in a menacing manner. A police officer is standing between them, trying not to look scared. He puts up his hands to stop them and says, "That's enough. I want you two groups to stay quite apart today. Or else . . ." One group leader steps forward and says, "Or else what?" and then looks around at the imagined huge crowd behind him. The other group leader steps forward and says to the policeman, "Yer, or else what . . .?" There is a pause as the audience considers the police officer's predicament. The old person shudders and wakes up and the 'ghosts of the past' melt away. She says, "Poor policeman. I wonder where he is now?" The old man opposite looks up. "I was that policeman," he says.

Now get the students to think of past events that might bring strong memories back for elderly people and get them to re-enact them.

AIM: To develop skills of interpretation and presentation in a dramatic form in the context of a mystery.

The teacher explains to the class that there has been a theft of a precious jewel from an isolated country manor and describes the scene of the crime. From walking in an empty space and pointing and describing well, the scene will come alive in the imaginations of the students. For example:

Over there is the safe that has been blown open by a small explosive. You can see the door hanging off its hinges. The jewel was in that safe and is now missing. Look over there, the guard dog is still sleeping off the effects of the drug it was somehow given. If you look at that window over there, just next to that massive oil painting you can see how the thief got in. As you know, we are three floors up so he must have been good at climbing and he probably used the drainpipe outside. We think the robbery happened late last night. Do you remember there was a terrific storm? We wonder how he managed to turn off the alarm. How did he know where the safe was? Interestingly he dropped his wallet and in it are some useful pieces of information. The occupants of the house were Lord and Lady Hamford and the butler and the maid. They were apparently all asleep when the theft took place.

After you have narrated the theft get the class to split up into small groups. Their task is to reconstruct and act out the theft from the night before.

EXTENSION IDEA

Ask students to think up their own crime scenes and then narrate these to the class. After each narration, the rest of the class can reconstruct the crime scene.

AIM: To develop the skill of presenting alternative viewpoints of an event.

SCENE 1

Get a group of four students to act out the following scenario:

> A group of amateur hillwalkers sets out in Scotland and is suddenly confronted with bad weather. An unexpected snowstorm rages and they are at high altitude and miles from anywhere. Incredibly they manage to use a mobile phone to get an emergency message through. They try to describe roughly where they are and then have to wait to be rescued in the freezing conditions.

SCENE 2

Get a group of three (pilot, navigator and winchman) to act out this scene:

> A helicopter rescue team is playing cards when the call comes through. They receive the call, run for the helicopter and then simulate the journey through the raging weather using thermal imaging cameras to locate the team in distress.

SCENE 3

This is the rescue scene itself, in which the students from scenes 1 and 2 work hard to add to the tension:

> The helicopter flies by the first time and then arrives again. The pilot manages to hover the helicopter low enough to bundle everyone onboard.

SCENE 4

Get students to play the part of parents whose mood changes from anxiety to relief:

> The parents are at home watching the news about the freak weather conditions and start to worry about their

children. A newsflash comes on about the rescue and then the news that they are safe and well.

SCENE 5

Get the pilot, a hillwalker, a parent and a student playing the part of a local police officer to say a few words to the TV cameras as follows:

- The helicopter pilot explaining how dangerous the flying conditions were.
- One of the rescued party explaining how the weather change was totally unexpected and how frightened they were.
- A parent saying how relieved she is to get them back.
- A police officer reminding hillwalkers always to take adequate precautions on walks like these.

EXTENSION IDEA

Get the groups to think up and work out their own rescue scenarios, remembering to consider a variety of viewpoints.

AIM: For students to develop skills of personification, gesture and sculpting by presenting the life of an inanimate object.

It helps if the students can prepare for this in advance of the lesson by choosing an inanimate object and sketching out its life history making sure that there are interesting facets and stages to act out. The activity works best if the student speaks for a short while about one life stage and then briefly acts out that stage.

Below is an example that can be given to one student to act out, with the inanimate object being a potato:

"I start my life as a tiny seed buried in the cold damp soil." (The student curls up and waits.) "Gradually I start to grow until my leaves open up to the sun." (The student could stretch out his arms and open up his hands as if they were leaves, and then pause for a few seconds.) "Eventually I'm dug up by a plough." (The student can leap up and then lie on the floor.) "Then I'm packed in a container with thousands of others." (The student stands up and then squeezes into a cramped position.) "I'm taken to a factory and washed." (The student acts out washing in a shower.) "I'm peeled." (The student acts out peeling off layers of skin.) "I'm chopped up into strange rectangular shapes and then sealed in an airtight plastic bag and frozen." (The student makes the shape of a frozen chip cramped in a bag.) "I stay like this, motionless for weeks." (The student stays in that position for a few moments looking forlorn.) "Eventually, the bag is cut open and light shines in!" (The student covers his eyes to show the brightness of the light.) "I then hear a sound like rustling leaves. Oh dear, it seems to be boiling oil." (The student looks scared as he is about to go into the chip pan.) "I'm fried to a lovely brown colour." (The student proudly presents his suntan, like a poser at the seaside.) "And now I'm being stabbed with a huge fork, dunked in some red sauce stuff and I'm heading towards a huge mouth . . ."

13

Improvisation

CROSSING THE ROOM

AIM: To practise a variety of ways to show movement individually and as part of a group.

Divide the class into two groups of equal size at either side of the acting area.

PHASE 1

Start the activity by telling one student to walk across to the other side as if he were a robot. Once he gets to the other side he points to a student and gives a command like 'old man'. That student then has to walk back across to the other side like an old man would. When he gets there he points to another student and gives another command like 'zombie' and so on. Let this run until lots of students have had a go.

PHASE 2

The two sides should now divide up into pairs. Start the activity again by picking one pair to walk across the room in the style of, for example, a tandem. One student must adopt a cycling position with another close behind him and together they 'ride' across the room. As before once they have got to the other side they should nominate a pair to go back using a different mode of 'transport'. Here are a few examples that have worked well for me:

○ tandem bicycle
○ motorbike and sidecar
○ wheelchair and pusher.

PHASE 3

This time the mode of transport across the area should be by way of groups of four students. Again, once they've crossed the space they should nominate a new group to travel back using a new method of transport.

Here are some examples for groups of four:

○ car
○ bus
○ horse and carriage
○ helicopter
○ ship.

AIM: To use skills of close observation and concentration.

Get the class to form a circle. A student is nominated (or a volunteer is chosen) and comes in to the centre of the circle. He invents a short sequence of actions. It is a good idea to start off with a simple sequence of actions and then become more adventurous as the activity develops. For example, a student may mime through the actions of opening a packet of cereal, pouring it into a bowl and adding milk and then stirring it. It works well if the sequence is about 15 to 20 seconds. The rest of the students have to watch the first run through carefully and then imitate the sequence of actions in unison. Try to keep the pace fairly slow and deliberate.

Run through the sequence two or three times. The first student then returns to the circle and another student comes to the centre and demonstrates his sequence. It can be the student next in the circle, or, in order to avoid putting a shy student on the spot, the teacher can choose randomly from volunteers.

If the students can't think of a sequence of actions, then suggest a few from the list below. It is best when one student follows another in quick succession but if it sags a little the teacher can bridge the gap with a few that he has prepared. It is important to keep the flow going. Here is a selection of sequences that work well:

o A shopkeeper arranging jewellery carefully on the shelves in the window of a shop.
o An actor taking a bow at the end of a performance.
o A football manager jumping up as his team scores.
o A teacher giving a look of fear, a frozen stance and then turning as if to run as she sees a giant snake enter the window of the classroom.

This activity develops concentration, allowing one student to take the limelight for a short time and then pass it on to the next student. The more willing students can of course come up with more than one sequence and the beauty is that even if certain students don't want to be the demonstrator they can still take an active part in the safety of the group.

AIM: To create a storyline from minimal information.

In life it is very common to pass someone in the street and hear a chance remark or a fragment of a conversation that leaves a sense of mystery and the merest glimpse of a life you've never known.

An interesting improvisation exercise is to start with such a fragment and use it as a stimulus to build a small play. It really does fire the creative imagination.

You will need a collection of chance remarks. It is best if the teacher provides these. Another way of coming up with raw material is to open a novel at random, place your finger on the page and use the first sentence you see. Here is an example fragment:

Well, to tell you the truth, I was thinking of dipping into some of the money my sister left me.

Certain questions are raised here, which you should discuss with the class, e.g. What is the money to be used for? How much? Why? Why did the sister leave the money? Were there conditions?

Once you've discussed these questions with the class, divide them into groups and get them to develop a small play based on their interpretation of the sentence. Below is a worked example of a discussion between two sisters:

"You know all those millions I made in business, Martha? Well, I've been thinking. I've been feeling a bit unwell lately and I've decided that I'm going to leave it all to you but on condition that if ever you see real need and want to help a worthy cause, then use it. But only use it for that."

Martha may reply, "Don't talk about such things Agnes. You've got years yet."

Years go by and sadly Agnes dies and leaves her money to Martha. One day Martha finds out that a local charity that serves soup to homeless people is to close through lack of funds. Martha offers not only to help but also to have a special modern homeless hostel built.

A representative from the charity says, "But, Martha, this will cost thousands. Can you afford it?"

Martha replies, "Well to tell you the truth, I was thinking of dipping into some of the money my sister left me."

AIM: For students to create their own ghost story.

Use the example below as a stimulus for students to work out their own 'strange meetings' with a ghost. Remind them that a scene is set by words, for example, "What brings you to this restaurant?"

It works well if the situation starts off as an ordinary scene and then slowly develops a ghostly angle, as in the example that follows.

DON'T I KNOW YOU?

The following conversation takes place between two people in a sweet shop.

Chris (to the assistant): "I'll have a bag of that fudge please."

Sarah: "Excuse me, but don't I know you from somewhere?"

Chris (looking intently): "I don't think so, no."

Sarah: "Yes I do. I remember . . . You were at my school. You were in my class, years ago, don't you remember?"

Chris: "Which school?"

Sarah: "Green Park, don't you remember? Old Skippy, our form teacher, you must remember him?"

Chris: "No, I don't remember him . . ." (There is a long pause. They look at each other.)

Sarah: "I've just thought of your name! It's Chris Lavender. You used to help me with my maths. Surely you remember that? I used to give you sweets for helping. You used to love . . . (pause) fudge . . ."

Chris: "Yes, my name is Chris Lavender, but I don't remember you."

Sarah: "Wait a minute, wait a minute." (Puts her head down in her hand as if deep in thought. Meanwhile Chris slowly edges away and disappears.) "I've got it. You were in all the newspapers. That's right. I've got it! You went missing. Assumed dead!" (Head comes up . . .) "It's great to see you after all this . . ."(She looks around. She is on her own.) "Chris? Chris? Where are you? Chris . . ."

AIM: For students to work together to create a mini-play from information provided by the teacher.

Prepare a set of cards with characters on one set, scenes on another, scenarios on another and 'lines to be incorporated' on the fourth set (see below for examples of content). It may take a bit of time to prepare but the payback is remarkable.

Divide the class into groups of five students and distribute the cards at random. Give each student a character card and a 'line to be incorporated' card. Give each group one scene card and one scenario card.

Ask the group to make a short play out of what they've been given. Allow some preparation time and then ask the groups to perform their plays to the rest of the class.

TIP: Colour code the cards and give as much advice and as many prompts as possible.

Remind the class that however strange their combinations may be, their job is to make the play as believable as possible. Here are some examples of cards:

CHARACTER CARD

Name: Steven

Age: 25

Background: Was in the army but now runs his own decorating business

Current mood: Irritated by everyone and shows it

Voice: Deep and loud

Habits: Keeps scratching his head and pointing in an intimidating way at people.

SCENE CARDS

Have cards for each of the following:

○ A hotel in Cairo in the middle of the night. It is very hot.

○ An igloo during a snowstorm.

○ A jungle full of dangerous animals.

o A desert at dawn.

o A mountain at dusk.

o A forest at midnight.

SCENARIO CARDS

Have one card for each of the following:

o An expensive ring has been stolen from one of the people.

o Someone is suddenly taken very ill.

o One person thinks he is being picked on.

'LINES TO BE INCORPORATED' CARDS

Have one card for each of the following:

o "Don't look at me like that!"

o "Well I've had enough of this. I'm going home."

o "What do you mean, there's an elephant coming towards us?"

AIM: To practise improvisation.

Divide the class into groups and give them different scenes to act out. These scenes should be seen as an opening to a longer play. Once the group has acted through the beginning they should then improvise how the scene progresses. It is useful to work through one example with the class and allow them to spend some time experimenting. Here are four examples:

SCENARIO 1: A POLICE STATION

A police officer is writing in his book at the desk of a police station. Suddenly a man bursts in, in a terrible state. The police officer looks up and asks him to calm down. The officer says, "You look to be in a terrible state, sir!" The man replies, "You'd be in this state too if you'd done what I just did! It's the most stupid mistake I've ever made in my life!" (students to continue . . .)

SCENARIO 2: A CLASSROOM

A lesson is in progress when suddenly the headteacher enters. She says to the class,

"We're very lucky today, class. You won't believe this! Look, we have a very, very special surprise visitor and he's got something for everyone." (students to continue . . .)

SCENARIO 3: A FRONT DOOR

Two officials knock on a person's front door. The householder opens the door.

The officers say, "We are sorry to disturb you. Have you heard what happened? Unfortunately you won't be able to live here anymore." (students to continue . . .)

SCENARIO 4: OUTSIDE A CINEMA

Someone is waiting for a friend outside the pictures. It is 15 minutes past the time arranged for the meeting. The person waiting is anxiously looking around. Suddenly the expected person arrives but says, "I'm sorry I'm late. I'm afraid I won't be able to see the film with you tonight because . . ." (students to continue . . .)

AIM: To develop the skills of listening, body memory and reaction.

Sit a group of eight students in a circle. Place an object in the centre, e.g. an ornament. The purpose of the object is to focus attention on the centre in almost a meditative way. Allow the students a few moments to look at the object and relax. Try to create a sense of 'expectancy'. This can work beautifully if the teacher walks around the outside edge of the circle and then in a quiet, soothing voice says things like, "Concentrate on the ornament. Block out all other thoughts. Just look at the ornament. Soon you will hear some sounds. Relax your body and wait, patiently. When you hear the sounds allow your body to react in some way. You may choose to ignore some sounds and others you may wish to show a reaction to. The important thing to remember is to react in the same way to the same sound."

Around the circle a larger circle forms with eight students. The outer circle will be standing, with a gap of at least a metre from the inner circle. Direct the activity with a soft soothing voice. Say things like, "Continue to look at the object. An outer circle has formed. Wait, in lovely silence. Now listen for the first sound and be ready to react, if you choose to." One of the students in the outer circle (standing) will make a noise, such as a clap. Allow take-up time. One (or more than one) of the students in the inner circle will react to the noise. Perhaps she will look around, or stand up or hold her head in her hands. Another outer circle student will then make a different noise, such as a low whistle and a different student in the inner circle will react in a different way (say, a hand up in the air for a fleeting moment). There then may be a pause, a short wait. Silence. All the inner students stare at the object in the centre of the circle. The teacher may then comment, "Good, some students have reacted. Other students have ignored these noises and are waiting for other noises. Continue to concentrate on the object. Now listen for some more noises." The teacher may then prompt a few more students in the outer circle to make new noises and so on.

After the students in the inner circle have reacted they can return to their pose of sitting and staring at the object in the centre of the circle.

The noises will continue. The important thing is to have a variety of noises. You may wish to use musical instruments or bells and a whole range of interesting sounds. You may wish to have a variety of rhythms, where the gaps and silences between the noises vary. Sometimes more than one student in the inner circle will react.

It is important for a pattern of reactions to be built up. If a clap causes a student in the inner circle to hold her head in her hands, for example, then each time the clap is heard the student must react in the same way. So students must remember what noise they heard and how they reacted to it. It may of course mean that certain noises produce a simultaneous reaction from, say, three different students. An interesting pattern of reactions will emerge.

The activity can be varied so that the students swap places between inner and outer circles and then the audience can have a go and the performers for the first part become the producers of noise for the next part.

To ensure a smooth and interesting activity you should be watching, monitoring and intervening to keep the action flowing.

AIM: To use the imagination to visualize and act out an amazing invention.

Discuss inventions with the group. First talk about real inventions that have made a difference to how we live today, e.g. light bulbs (it works well if the examples are in the room you are teaching in). Then talk about inventions they would like to see that would make their lives easier. Then divide the students into small groups. Each group should think up their own amazing invention and set up a play to show how the invention will work. You could use the idea below as an example to get them started:

> An inventor has come up with an amazing 'Duplicating Machine'. A student (acting the mad professor type) introduces the machine to a would-be purchaser.

For preparation you will need a selection of pairs of objects, for example, two apples, two coins, two blank exercise books, two spoons, two identical textbooks etc. The inventor says (with great excitement), "This has taken me 20 years to develop but here it is at last! My amazing duplicating machine! It will duplicate anything. Look!" The demonstrator then takes an apple and places it in 'pod 1' (a space on the floor). He presses a 'button' (a science fiction soundtrack is useful here for a few seconds). Then a duplicate of the object arrives in 'pod 2' (another space on the floor nearby where the teacher places the paired object).

Run this through a few times using ever more elaborate and different objects and the would-be purchaser becomes more and more amazed and excited! She can't wait to buy it.

Then the question is posed: "Will it duplicate a person?" The answer is "Yes" and then you get two students to play their parts. When they emerge from the 'pods' one must copy the other! It is great if they can be holding the same thing to add a little authentication!

AIM: Turning a routine activity into a sudden emergency.

SCENE: AN ORDINARY DAY AT WORK AT THE OFFICE

As a warm-up allow a few students to enter as office workers and do the sorts of things they would do in an office. Here is a prompt list of the activities they could choose:

o unlocking filing cabinets
o switching on computers
o opening post
o picking up and looking in folders
o asking each other how they are.

Allow this sequence to run until the group of, say, five students is happy with the routine. Then explain that when you run the sequence, one of the office workers will stop and stare at a 'dangerous creature' that is in the room. Various decisions need to be made, such as:

o Where in the room will the animal be?
o What will it be?
o What will it be doing?

The worker who sees it is clearly petrified. She tries to attract the attention of her colleagues. It may take a while for it to dawn on everyone what is happening.

What will they say? How will they move? Perhaps by backing out slowly with a look of horror as they stare at the creature?

EXTENSION IDEA

Students can develop their own scenarios where an ordinary situation suddenly becomes terrifying in some way (it doesn't have to be a dangerous animal).

THE DANGEROUS ANIMAL

IDEA

20

AIM: To visualize strange images from dreams and respond with spontaneous body sculptures to unusual and surreal instructions.

PREPARATION

The students work in pairs to discuss dreams they have had.

Once a dream has been selected, one student stands on his own in the centre of the space. He starts by saying, "Let me tell you about the dream I had last night."

There are two main methods. In the first, he can explain what happened and stare into space saying how clear the strange images were. Keep it short, say, about two minutes. In the second, have the student explain the images clearly and slowly, pausing after each image.

A group of, say, three students then act out in mime the images and hold human statue shapes to illustrate the images of the dream.

After each image allow time for the students to melt smoothly into a 'neutral position' ready for the next image. Here are some examples that you could try to get warmed up with:

○ "In my dream a giant was plodding towards me . . ."
○ "In my dream a special person I hadn't seen for years emerged from the mist and just stood there . . ."
○ "In my dream I could dance brilliantly and people applauded . . ."

Then encourage students to experiment with their own ideas.

EXTENSION IDEA

Music and sound effects can be added to highlight the impact of the images.

AIM: To read significance into an object and produce a 'shared dramatic memory'.

For this idea to work well, it will need a little bit of preparation. Ask each student to bring into the next lesson a short extract of music and an important object. The object and the music are chosen from an important moment in the student's life. For example, a movie ticket may remind her of a night out with a boyfriend; a toy may remind him of his nan; a feeding bowl may remind her of a pet that has sadly now died, and so on.

The music must have an important significance in their lives and they will give a short introduction to it. The object will be for the audience to focus on while the music is playing.

The idea is to show the dramatic impact that music and an object can have when the audience 'reads' significance into it. For example, students may play part of one of their songs, for one minute. On a table in the centre of the empty acting space they may place a bottle of coconut suntan lotion.

Before the music begins they give a short introduction. The student does not have to say too much about it. Carefully spoken hints, perhaps adding emotion in the voice, can create the effect. So they may say, "This music takes me back two years to my wonderful holiday in Spain. When I smell the coconut suntan lotion and hear this song I think of yellow sands and blue seas. I met a really nice person on this holiday. I can see his face in my imagination and I remember his huge smile. I wonder where he is now."

The music is then played for a short time and everyone looks at the object. It becomes a shared dramatic memory. It is amazing how the drama lifts off in the imagination of the audience as significance is added to the music and the object in a magical way.

It is a good idea if the students can run through what they are going to say at home beforehand. Students love doing this one as it gives them a chance to share something special in a dramatic and unusual way.

THE MUSIC AND THE OBJECT

THE SECRET MAGIC DIARY

AIM: To develop the skill of using acting flashbacks.

As a homework activity, ask the students to write down a diary of interesting events that have happened in the past. During the lesson, divide the class into groups. One person reads out the diary and the others in the group act out the scenes. Alternatively, or in addition, you could prepare a few diary entry ideas of your own. Here is a worked example. You could use this to illustrate the idea before the students write their own diaries.

SCENE: AN OLD HOUSE

A couple of people are cleaning things up after the previous owner has passed away. One of them comes across a diary. She reads the front cover, which says, 'Secret, magic diary. My life'. They discuss whether or not to open and read it. They decide that they will.

They open it, slowly. (It would be useful for a strange bit of background music to create a bit of spooky atmosphere as it is opened.)

One of them reads the first page: "This is my life. It will be magically summoned up if you read it with interest."

The page is turned and one of them reads, "When I was born I nearly died. I was put to one side, on a table."

The people look up as, slowly, two actors appear in the room and act out and improvise the scene just after the birth. One of them is a midwife and shakes her head to say that the poor thing will never survive. She acts out placing the baby to one side. The people who discovered the diary look at each other in amazement. One of them urges the other to turn the page and read on.

The next page describes the first day at school and again it is acted out in front of them.

The diary continues throughout her life and each time the actors act out the scene. Keep the acting flashbacks quite short and develop a rhythm in the timing of the reading with the actors bringing the past to life. Practise the matching and timing of the reading to the acting.

TIP: Remind the actors acting out the events to be completely absorbed in them and not to communicate in any way with the reader of the diary. They are 'visions'.

THE STRANGE STICKS

AIM: To explore what can happen when time freezes.

The strange sticks have amazing power. When they are tapped together three times everyone freezes in time for exactly one minute. The person who taps them is not frozen and can do whatever he wants. What fun he could have!

Ask students to work out little scenes where one of them can tap the sticks. For example:

A student is being cornered by a group of ruffians. They creep menacingly towards him saying things like, "Come on, hand over your money!" The student with the two sticks warns them off by saying, "Clear off or you'll be sorry!"

They laugh at him. Suddenly he taps the sticks together and the group freezes. While they are frozen he has fun laying them down on the ground, taking off their ties and binding their hands and feet. A minute passes and a sound signifies that everything is back to normal. Of course the group of ruffians struggle helplessly on the floor while the possessor of the sticks walks off saying, "I warned you!"

Ask students to work out in their groups interesting situations where the use of such sticks would produce dramatic interest.

AIM: To develop the skill of creating believable truth in drama.

PREPARATION

Ask students to sit in pairs and think up ordinary things that have happened to them. Then ask them to add on an unbelievable event. Allow them about ten minutes to do this and then begin the acting activity.

Seat the class in a circle and ask a volunteer to stand in the middle of the circle. This student should talk through their unbelievable event as if it were completely ordinary. After they have finished their account the class should question the student and the student should try and answer them in a convincing and realistic way. For example:

I was swimming today at the leisure centre, having a great time when a giant octopus suddenly started attacking everyone in the pool. It wrapped one of its huge tentacles around me and tried to drag me under the water. But I was having none of it. I bit it so hard that it let go. Then I chased it out of the swimming pool. It ran really fast. It was scared you know. Then I shouted, "And don't come back." Everybody clapped. I carried on swimming.

TIP: You should have ready a few examples of surreal events and be prepared to tell these if the students seem to be getting stuck.

THE WEATHER METER

AIM: To show rapid reactions to physical weather conditions.

This is a great warm-up activity. The students find a space. The teacher announces a scale of 1 to 10. Explain that we are going to explore how temperatures affect the way we move. Get them to walk slowly around the space being careful not to bump into anybody. The temperature is now at 5 which is normal room temperature and perfectly comfortable, while 10 is the hottest part of the Sahara Desert and 0 is the North Pole. As they move slowly around, start increasing or lowering the temperature as signified by the number called out. Give them take-up time to adjust their reactions to the changing temperatures.

You can repeat the exercise with other aspects of weather and severity on a scale of 1 to 10. You could, for example, use wind speeds, rain and thickness of fog. It's great fun.

Remind students that although there are many of them in the room, they must focus only on themselves for this to work well.

AIM: To explore and act out a dramatic predicament.

Ask students to find a partner. Place them in a difficult 'what if' situation and ask them to act out and discuss what they would do to get out of the situation. Get someone to introduce and explain their predicament before the acting begins. For example:

INTRODUCTION

"Two people were walking through the countryside when they fell down a disused well. They both have injured ankles. There is a little bit of light."

A: "What on earth are we going to do?"

B: "My ankle hurts."

A: "So does mine. But how are we going to get out of here?"

B (looking around with a scared expression): "We must have fallen down an old well or something. Shall we shout for help?"

A: "No, we're miles away from anywhere. No one will hear us."

B: "We've got to try something."

A: "How about trying to climb out?"

B (reaching to the walls): "No, it would be useless. These bricks are crumbling to pieces. This must be really old."

A (getting angry): "But why wasn't there a proper cover on it?"

B: "I don't know . . ."

And so on. Get students to work out their own 'what if' predicaments in this way and practise them and then perform them to the rest of the class.

TIP: It works particularly well if the teacher has some 'what if' situations already typed out on cards.

Characters and Lives

CHARACTER PROFILES

AIM: To allow students to adopt a character and explore that character by 'hot-seating'.

Ask six students to stand in a line a little bit apart from each other, facing the rest of the class. Allocate each student a number and allocate a character to each number. For example:

1 an old man
2 a busy working mum
3 a teenager
4 a nine-year-old girl
5 a very wealthy man of 50
6 a circus strongwoman of 25.

Now the rest of the class fire short questions, one at a time, at the characters. For example:

o "Number 1, what is your favourite food?" The old man will reply, in role, with the typical type of food he might like, e.g. "Beef stew."
o "Number 4, what are your favourite clothes?" Reply: "A pink dress."
o "Number 5, what car do you drive?" Reply: "A Bentley."
o "Number 3, what is your favourite music?" Reply: "Slipknot."

And so on.

TIPS: The key is to keep it brisk (with the teacher filling the gaps to prevent slack if necessary) and for the characters to respond in role with the answers that they think would be appropriate for that particular character. Once several questions have been fired, swap around the students. Think of allocating different characters.

The good thing about this idea is that it puts students into character immediately and 'hot-seats' them. It forces the student to learn to think like the character they have adopted.

AIM: To invent characters and then scenarios in which those characters can act.

Divide the class into two groups. Each group will invent a character and choose a student to play that character. For example, the first group may invent a man whose clothes are scruffy and whose voice is angry, who is a highly emotional genius. They should also invent some background information about him, e.g. he may have had a nervous breakdown, or he may have been wealthy and gambled all his money away.

The second group may invent a woman who can't go into a shop without stealing things. She has been to prison. She had an accident years ago which meant she can no longer use her left arm and it hangs loosely to her side.

After this preparation stage, the two characters step out into the acting area and each group introduces their character. Choose a student from either group and ask him to come up with a scenario, for example:

> It is late at night on an otherwise deserted railway station. The two characters are strangers and are waiting for the last train. One of them is feeling a little scared and nervous. The other notices this. A conversation begins . . .

The two students should then invent a dialogue between the two characters based on how they think their character would act in this situation.

Once they have acted this out, get the students to invent more and unusual characters and put them together in more unusual situations.

COMPOSITE CHARACTERS

AIM: To focus on the dramatic impact of a meeting between two characters who grew up together but who now lead entirely different lives.

Two people grew up together at school and became great friends. After leaving school they lost contact with each other. One of them joined a band and after a few years became rich and famous. The other leads an ordinary life. One day, four years after leaving school, they meet by chance. This activity focuses on the dramatic impact of a meeting between them where their differing circumstances come together.

You can use this mini-script and then continue it or think up your own scenario and improvise the conversation that the characters might have. The fact that one of them is now rich and famous has a huge impact on the conversation. Here is an example of a scene:

SETTING

A supermarket, very late at night. There are not many other people about.

A: "Is that you Barry?"

B: "Jolene? I don't believe it. How are you?"

A: "Fine." (awkward silence) "I've heard about you. You're on the telly all the time." (awkward silence) "I saw you on Top of the Pops last week."

B: "Yer, we've been lucky I suppose." (awkward silence) "What are you up to?"

A: "I work in a shop."

B: "Which one?"

A: "Oh, just Woolworth's. It's not exciting." (awkward silence)

B: "Do you remember when we used to go to the movies together?"

A: "Of course I do." (awkward silence) "Are you married or anything?"

B: "No. Are you?"

A: "No."

B: "Are you doing anything later tonight?" (awkward silence) "Come over to my place for a drink if you like."

A: "Where?"

B: "I'll send a car for you."

Get the students to act out alternative conversations of old friends who meet up years after they last saw one another and whose lives have gone in different directions.

AIM: For the students to focus on the reaction of characters to their own private thoughts echoed back to them.

Stand the class in a circle. A student is going to be singled out, and stand in the centre of a circle, to demonstrate what his thoughts are. The method used here is for him to voice his thoughts and for the others (the circle of students) to echo them back to represent the processes, within his mind, and the effects his thoughts have on his emotions. Normally a person's private thoughts can only be guessed at by what that person says. Here we take the process dramatically one step further. When the words are echoed back, they represent the reflective time we experience in our mind when we think something and become aware of all of that thought's associations. The person in the circle reacts to the echo to amplify and show the effect his own thoughts are having on him.

A volunteer stands in the circle. He says words and little phrases and short sentences from any part of his life. For example:

"First day at school I won a sweet."

The line is picked up and repeated back by a few people (say four) around the circle. They will say the same words, yet vary their delivery, maybe altering the volume, speed, mood or emphasis etc.

The volunteer will continue, keeping the lines short and adopting a rhythm of utterance, pause and then echoes. During the echoes he will listen and think. For example, he may say: "I should have gone on that camping trip!" The words may be whispered back by, say, three students in the circle: "I should have gone on that camping trip . . . I should have gone on that camping trip . . ." As the words are whispered back, the student in the centre of the circle will adopt an expression of listening to the echoes, as if they are thoughts, and will then react to them. He may put his head in his hands and keep perfectly still. He might decide to punch the air with an angry expression. The echoed voices will then cease. He will stand up again and say something else. Once again it will be echoed back, this time perhaps in a shouting voice. He may move around the circle but always he will listen to those echoes. His facial expressions may change as he hears the echoes to show his reflective thoughts.

The next person will get up after a few thoughts and the first person will join the circle and the process continues. The utterances can be from any part of life and could be very significant or seemingly trivial. For example:

- "I met a famous footballer, he shook my hand . . ."
- "I miss that pet, I really do."
- "Why did I do that? Why?"

It doesn't matter if there's mystery or incompleteness attached to some as this creates interesting effects. The dramatic interest is contained in the way the character reacts to his reflected thoughts rather than in the audience knowing the full story.

For example, he may say: "One more mark and I would have passed . . ." This will be echoed back and he will react. He may look downcast and walk slowly with slumped shoulders. The imagination of the audience will be working away, thinking about and creating a context for this snippet of information.

AIM: To develop the skill of dramatic description.

INTRODUCTION

An eccentric millionaire has organized a competition where he will give a prize of a free holiday to anyone who, in one minute with a dramatic description, can describe where and why they would like to go.

PRACTICE PREPARATION SESSION

Ask the students to think of somewhere nice where they would like to go on holiday and suggest reasons why it might be a great place to visit. For example: "I would love to visit Spain to swim in the warm sea and sample the exotic food; I would love to visit America and see where they make the films; I would love to visit Canada and have a go at canoeing in the great rivers . . ." Allow five minutes for the students to experiment in pairs and then announce that the competition is to begin.

When several students are happy with their ideas they can progress to the next stage.

THE SET UP

One student plays the part of the eccentric millionaire. He sits in a chair and the students who have chosen to enter the competition form a queue. Make sure there is plenty of space in front of the millionaire.

The millionaire has an assistant who ushers people in. It would be helpful if she could refer to a notebook or clipboard. The assistant will announce the 'contestant' and time him for one minute.

The announcement could be something like: "Here is the next contestant. His name is Gary Tomlin and he is going to describe why he wants to go to Hawaii!" Build up some excitement with perhaps rising inflection in the announcement. "Gary, best of luck, you have one minute starting now . . ."

The student will then describe with words and using the excitement in his tone, movements and gestures why he would like to go there. The rest of the class will be the audience. For example:

"I want to go to Hawaii because I can't wait to surf on the world's best waves!" (He will then pull a posture of a surfer.) "The palm trees will sway in the cool breeze." (He will then adopt the shape of a tree and sway gently and smile. He will continue with images and illustrate them dramatically until one minute is up.)

It works better if the rhythm is brisk.

After several contestants have performed, stop the contest and ask the millionaire to decide who the winner is. It is a good idea to have a limit on how many entries there are, for example, seven, to keep the momentum tight.

THE HOLIDAY FROM HELL

AIM: To reconstruct and act out the tensions of a customer versus company complaint situation.

BACKGROUND INFORMATION

A group of holidaymakers have arrived at the head office of Star Dream Holidays. The managing director has agreed to speak to them. They are deeply unhappy about their experiences and are going to explain what they are unhappy about and then they will demand a refund and compensation. They have been to Spain and report the following things that they are unhappy about:

- The flight was delayed by one day.
- The coach broke down on the way to the hotel and all the tourists had to walk the remaining 2 miles carrying heavy cases in blistering heat.
- The staff at the hotel were rude.
- The food was disgusting.
- The bedrooms were appalling. There were insects in the bed linen.

Students can try to add ideas to this list as to what went wrong. The rules of the complaints procedure are that only one person may speak at a time.

The following characters are required:

- The managing director
- The managing director's assistant
- Security staff (two or three)
- Angry customers (between five and ten).

SET UP

Arrange the managing director standing at one end of the performance area with his assistant next to him and the security guards flanking either side.

The customers are led in and seated in a row with 3 metres separating them from the managing director. One by one the customers explain the problem in detail, either thinking up their own complaint or embellishing one from the ideas list. The managing director remains calm and always has an answer to the problem. He tries to twist things around so that they don't sound too bad. For example:

Customer: "Our coach broke down and we had to walk in the blazing heat all the way to the hotel carrying our heavy cases."

Managing director: "Come on. Come on. Look on the bright side. You had lovely sunshine and a nice walk in the fresh air. It's a good way to get to see the countryside. In a coach you just flash past and don't see anything. Next complaint please . . ."

TIPS: Encourage the students to express themselves clearly. The customers must remain seated, and if the managing director asks to go on to the next customer then they must comply with that. Having such rules prevents the arguments from getting out of hand.

THE INSPECTOR

AIM: To explore reactions to officially important people.

Set up a demonstration group of, say, five students and allocate them a job each on a building site. One may be laying bricks, another may be plastering a wall and so on. Allow them to work through a short sequence of typical actions for the job they are miming. Remind them about precision of movement and suitable pace of actions. The really important focus is a relaxed easy routine and flow of movement that would be expected from someone who carries out this work all the time.

Space out the students in such a way as to give an idea of the size of the site. Run through the sequence a couple of times until it flows nicely.

A building inspector unexpectedly arrives with his clipboard. His self-importance causes the builders to carry on with their work, but with more tension and a wary eye on the inspector. He asks who is in charge and one of the students shows him around. He stops and looks at aspects of the work and makes officious comments like, "Em, that plaster looks a bit dodgy!" or, "Why isn't he wearing a safety hat?" For each thing he sees he jots down a note on his clipboard accompanied with tuts etc.

Eventually he leaves and we see a huge release of tension in the workers who make comments poking fun at the inspector.

The next step is for the students to get into groups of about five and work out scenarios where an inspector can suddenly arrive and find fault. For example, a kitchen, a factory production line, a shop, a swimming pool. Appoint one student for each group to oversee and direct it for a short performance. Each group can then perform to the rest of the class.

AIM: To explore how a sudden change in circumstances can change a power relationship between two people.

Give the scenario below to your class. You'll need the following actors:

○ A narrator
○ Mr Henshaw – a mild-mannered man
○ Mr Bull – Mr Henshaw's aggressive boss
○ A receptionist
○ Mr Snoop – a private detective.

A narrator introduces Mr Henshaw. He is working in an office. Mr Bull charges in and shouts angrily at him, "Why haven't you done this? Why haven't you done that? Tidy this place up, it's a disgrace!" and similar words.

Mr Henshaw cowers at his desk, fumbling with his paperwork. Mr Bull stands over him and glares down, accusing him of wasting time. Mr Henshaw tries to speak but is told to shut up and get on. Mr Bull storms off shouting, "If things don't improve you're sacked, sunshine!"

Mr Henshaw pulls out his diary and writes in it. The narrator explains to the audience: "When Mr Henshaw became very stressed last year, he visited a stress counsellor who suggested that he recorded his thoughts and feelings in a diary." The narrator then watches Mr Henshaw write in the diary. The narrator speaks as he writes: "Dear diary, Mr Bull is becoming impossible. Everything I do is wrong. I'm also worried about the debts at home. They're mounting up. Debt collectors called last night and took my telly! What am I going to do?"

A receptionist comes in and hands Mr Henshaw a letter saying, "A letter, special delivery for you, Mr Henshaw! Oh, and this is Mr Snoop. Apparently he's a private detective."

Mr Henshaw looks puzzled and opens and reads the letter. The narrator speaks while he reads: "Dear Mr Henshaw, as solicitors acting for your late great aunt,

Miss Daisy May Henshaw deceased, I have the duty to inform you that her will has now been read and proved and you are to inherit one million pounds forthwith subject to a small condition. I quote from the will: 'Donald, I'm happy for you to have this money but I've appointed a private detective to check that you comply with just one small condition of the inheritance. It is this: don't allow people to walk all over you ever again! Your loving Great Aunt.'"

The class should improvise what happens when Mr Bull returns. As an alternative to improvisation, small rehearsal groups can be set up to work out alternative ways of developing the scene.

TIP: It works particularly well if Mr Henshaw asserts himself gradually as Mr Bull has no knowledge that he has no effective power over his employee anymore.

AIM: To develop reactions to people.

INTRODUCTION

This exercise will explore how ordinary people react in subtle and obvious ways to the presence of a famous person.

PREPARATORY EXERCISE

Arrange the group around the room in a random way. Pick volunteers, one at a time, to play the part of a famous person and to saunter around chatting to people. Try this for a minute or so with everyone ignoring the famous person.

Then try it again with everyone staring at the famous person and watching them as they walk around. Focus on the idea of the way people react to a famous person and make that person the centre of attention. Now try the following scene:

o One student plays the part of the monarch.
o A few students play the part of waiters and waitresses who bring around trays of drinks and sandwiches.
o The other students play the part of guests, grouped about in a garden party.

Arrange groups of three and four people around the room. Their activity is to hold drinks, sip away and nibble on sandwiches and chat very quietly to each other. The 'monarch' walks around slowly and chats to different groups. When the monarch arrives at a group the rest of the group must make him the centre of attention. The other groups have to keep an awareness of where the monarch is. As the monarch gets closer they react more intensely. For example:

o They may position their bodies to get a better view of the monarch.
o They may be talking to someone but looking over their shoulders so that their attention is on the monarch.

THE ROYAL GARDEN PARTY

- ○ Their body language may become edgy and nervous.
- ○ They may be a little stunned and not sure quite what to do.
- ○ They may act in a slightly odd way, like looking at their shoes and then suddenly looking at the monarch.

AIM: To present key points of an event dramatically, using human statues and minimal words.

Get your students to imagine the following situation:

> A man is on a beach on a hot summer's day. He hires a deckchair. He puts it on the beach and puts his hands around the main joints beneath his seat. The chair collapses without warning, trapping his hands in the joints of the wood. His hands and fingers are seriously damaged.

This event will have a ripple effect of consequences and this can be represented by a series of statues. For each posture, go through the following routine: hold the position for a count of five; say the words; return to the position for another count of five. The following is an example of the first three statues of a series:

1 Stands with his hands held together. He stares down at the hands. Then he says: "For years later all I could think about were my hands. Yes they did get better slowly but you wouldn't believe how much you use them . . ."

2 Stands slightly bent over, pointing. "I still hire out deckchairs but you can imagine how I warn everyone to be careful where they put their hands."

3 Stands with head in hands. "I was the one who unpicked his hands from the broken deckchair. I still wake up in the night seeing them there, all crushed. I can't get the screaming out of my head . . . it was horrible . . . horrible."

And so on.

Now ask students to think up an event and then represent the ripple effect of the event with statues representing a variety of viewpoints.

IDEA

37

THE SUITCASE

AIM: To imagine and reconstruct in the mind a character from the clues of his possessions.

This activity will require one suitcase as a prop.

STEP 1

There is a conversation between a hotel porter and the hotel manager over a suitcase that has been left in one of the rooms. Over a week has gone by and they have been unable to contact the owner. The decision is made to open the case.

STEP 2

With difficulty and using various tools the porter is able to open the case. The first thing they bring out is a notebook. It is opened and read: "I have been followed for over a year now. I am at the Hotel Rembrando and it is time to change my identity."

The next item brought out is a small painting covered in a cloth. When they take the cloth off they let out a yell. It is an original Van Gogh.

More and more items are brought out of the case. The items could be actual props or they could be imagined and made up. If they are made up and therefore the action is mimed, then the way the student handles and describes them is crucial. For example, she may say: "Look at this," as she lifts it out and unwraps it slowly. "Oh the smell!" She pokes at it carefully. "It looks like a sandwich of ham that has been discarded for months! See how the bread has changed to dust and powder."

A good way to ensure that the students do not run out of ideas is for the teacher to have a list of items in the suitcase written up on the whiteboard with a few hints on how they could be described.

Ask students to continue this, each item throwing more light onto the life of this mysterious character.

Eventually stop the activity and ask the students to reflect and imagine what the person who owned that suitcase was like. The students can also be asked to imagine the circumstances of his life at the point where the case was left at the hotel. It is amazing to see how these possessions can create a powerful image in your students' minds.

Exploring
the World

COURT CASE

AIM: To act out a court case showing how behaviour is affected by conventions.

This works best if you develop a case that could be taken to court. For example, a person may be injured on a zebra crossing by a bus. A case is brought against the bus driver for negligence. The driver maintains that the plaintiff ran out without warning and he had no time to stop. In the courtroom you will need the following people:

- judge (works well if the teacher takes this part to direct the proceedings. When she says, "Silence in court!" it has a great impact!)
- prosecution lawyer
- defence lawyer
- defendant (bus driver)
- plaintiff (person knocked down)
- witnesses (about four who saw what happened)
- doctor (to give evidence about the injuries)
- manager of bus depot (to give a character reference for the bus driver)
- jury (twelve people who decide on the verdict once they've heard the case)
- the public gallery (those left who don't want to take an active part and simply watch).

Keep to simplified forms of protocol for a court, e.g. when the judge enters, everyone stands. Other examples of court protocol and procedures are:

- The judge's word is final. If anyone argues, the judge can hold them 'in contempt of court' and have them removed and even jailed.
- There will be a gallery for the general public who may watch but may not interfere in any way with the proceedings.
- At the beginning of the case the judge will read out the charge to the defendant. Make it sound formal, e.g. "John Taylor, you are charged with negligence,

that on 1 August 2007 you did drive a bus in Norwich and did knock down and injure the plaintiff Alison Ducksbury. How do you plead, guilty or not guilty?"

o The prosecution and defence lawyers will get opportunities to put their cases and call and question witnesses. A good way to start the questioning is to say (once the name and address is confirmed), "Can you tell the court in your own words what you saw?"

o Remember that the court deals only in facts and not opinions (unless it is a 'professional' opinion).

o At the end of the trial the jury will retire to decide their verdict and then this will be formally asked for by the judge (appoint a spokesperson for the jury).

o The judge will pass down the sentence or if the accused is acquitted he will be formally told that he is free to go.

Arrange the space with a 'witness box' and the defence and prosecution tables facing each other with plenty of empty space in the middle. The lawyers can walk around the space saying things like: "Now, Mr Smith, in your own words can you tell the court what happened on that day?" You can either allow the court case to develop organically as the students improvise or you can write a script for the students to follow.

AIM: To bring a photograph alive dramatically.

You will need to have a selection of photographs collected from a variety of sources including magazines. These can be found in all sorts of books. For example:

○ pictures of firemen by their engine
○ a scene of an old rambling country house
○ a forest scene with lumberjacks at work
○ a factory with rows of workers by their machines
○ a historic photo of an Edwardian house with aristocratic people and their servants all together in a group photo.

Divide the class into smaller groups of four or five and give each group a photograph to work with. One of the group is nominated as a director and arranges the students to represent characters and inanimate objects shown in the picture. The group then look at the picture and make up an imaginary story based on the picture.

The group reassemble to represent the picture and allow a pause while they keep still. This is the freeze frame. Then one by one the students tell their story. While one student is talking (and animating his talk with gestures and facial expressions), the others keep still in their positions in the 'picture'. Allow about a minute for the character to give his talk. Then he steps back into the 'picture', allows a small pause and then another character comes alive and tells his story.

When this group has completed its performance, another group will present another 'picture' with its story to tell. Here is an example based on a photograph showing some farmers having their lunch around an old tractor in a field in summertime. The scene is from the year 1910. The farmers can be played by students A, B and C and the tractor by a student known as D:

A (stepping forward 'out of the picture'): "Hallo. My name is William. I'm enjoying this cheese sandwich. I've had nothing since five this morning. I'm famished. It's hard work, up and down the field all day. Ploughing and ploughing! You sweat like anything in this heat! Tonight I shall drag myself to the tavern and have a few pints of cider. I shall then go home and fall fast asleep. Tomorrow it all begins again! Still, as my old nan used to say, God bless her, 'You're lucky to have a job William, that you are!'" He then takes up his position again in the 'picture' and holds a still pose while the next character steps forward. This time it is the tractor.

D: "I wonder when these farmers are going to give my old engine a service. I'm burning black sooty oil and I'm feeling the strain at my age. Up and down the fields all day and I've been doing this now for 15 years! I suppose I'll end up on the scrap heap like all my old friends. Then it's a worry. People will start to pinch stuff off me. A tyre here, a steering wheel there, maybe even a bit of my old rusty bodywork. Before you know it I'll be a few nuts and bolts on the soil. Still, mustn't get sad, there's still work to be done!"

The great thing about this idea is that you can create a variety of situations and moods and atmospheres. Returning to the freeze frame picture gives the activity an 'anchor' to work around.

CAVE DWELLERS

AIM: To act out a scene from prehistory using improvising skills and conjecture.

The teacher sets the scene. He tells the group that they are to imagine that it is thousands of years ago and they are early people living in a cave. By a miracle of modern technology a person from today is able to go back in time and witness what these early people are doing and then comment on the action for a television audience. They are to divide up into groups of four. Three will be the actors and one will be the 'time travel' narrator, or rather commentator.

The groups can then experiment with everyday imagined activities of the cave dwellers. They will communicate with grunts, strange sounds and gestures. The commentator will then comment on what he sees and interpret it for his modern audience.

For example, one group may be making a fire. One may be gathering wood while another rubs sticks to produce a spark. The commentator may say, "This cavewoman is tidying up the cave while the man is rubbing sticks to make the spark. Notice that the fire is placed at the entrance to this cave. I can see one of their children over there collecting wood for the fire. It is very smelly in here. Look there is the hog they've caught and killed ready to be cooked."

The careful improvised actions of the actors together with the commentary produce a strong imaginative scene.

Other groups can experiment with other suggested activities of the cave dwellers. When they are ready they can display a few scenes to the rest of the group. Here are a few suggestions for activities of the cave dwellers:

o cutting down trees and working the wood
o fishing by the side of the river
o chipping flints (flint napping)
o making weapons
o making animal traps.

AIM: To work out in groups an imaginative adventure and show dramatically how the problems encountered are dealt with.

Arrange the class into groups of five. Give each an exotic location to explore.

Choose from Egypt and the Pyramids, the dense jungle, the middle of the ocean on a ship, a mountain range, a deep cave or Antarctica.

Their mission is to explore the area and report back to the rest of the group to explain what conditions were like.

STEP 1

Each group is to sit in a circle and discuss the sorts of problems that they are likely to encounter in their particular location. For example, in the dense jungle travelling would be heavy going because of thick vines, the air would be humid and heavy, sweat would be a problem, they would need lots of water, and storing and carrying food would be a problem, as would finding shelter, dangerous insects and snakes.

STEP 2

The group work out what would be needed in their rucksacks.

STEP 3

The group act out key points of the adventure, which might involve how progress was made, how food was found and cooked, how water was found and how shelter was made, and then how these various dangers were faced and overcome.

STEP 4

The students should then decide on the significant events that happen during the adventure. Consider the key points of the expedition.

Each group now appoints a narrator. The group stand in front of the rest of the class and the narrator explains how the expedition went. He will show the class some key points, as if they are watching a video. He will introduce them and then allow the other members of the group to act out the key scenes. For example:

"We made good progress on the first day but halfway through day two when we tried to rest we encountered a rather nasty problem." The group then act out a scene where they are trying to rest but they realize that thousands of soldier ants are swarming everywhere on the ground. One of the team shows them how to make hammocks and secure them high above the ground.

Each group must show the key points of the expedition to the rest of the class by a combination of narration and acting.

AIM: For students to act out the typical actions of various jobs.

Ask the students to walk slowly around the space being careful not to bump into each other. The teacher then announces the names of different jobs and the students must walk and act in the typical way in which the people who do those jobs usually walk. Here are a few prompts:

○ a soldier (students may march)
○ a traffic warden (students may get out a notebook and lean over to read a number plate)
○ a labourer digging a trench in the road (using his spade and showing signs of physical strain).

The next step is to explore a particular job in more detail. For example, if we consider a museum security guard:

○ How would he walk?
○ How would he look around?
○ When he stops to look at an exhibit, how would he look at it (remembering that he has done this thousands of times)?
○ In what ways would he show boredom?

Ask for two or three volunteers to come up and show the group how they might act out the things on the prompt list. At this stage break down the behaviour into little detailed chunks.

Now split the class into groups of four and allocate a choice of three jobs for each group. Allow them some practice time to work out how to move about and act characteristically for that particular job. To help in this part it's a good idea to have prompt cards prepared that will detail types of job, key questions to consider about the job and typical activities to act out.

Finally ask each group to act out their jobs and get the others to guess what they are.

AIM: To present from a variety of viewpoints differing emotions and experiences by people who are all working on the same project.

Choose nine students to stand in a line facing the rest of the class. Assign them each a character and allow them time to think about how their character would act and then ask them to perform it to the class.

The worked example below shows the different emotions of the various characters half an hour before a play is about to start. Using body language, facial expressions and tone of voice the characters express how they are feeling:

A member of the audience: "I'm really excited and looking forward to it! I can't wait to see the star! I've waited ages!" (She might show her excitement by the way she rapidly turns the programme around in her hands.)

The box office manager: "Nobody would see any star without us! It's been so hectic. Loads of people scrambling to get their hands on last-minute tickets! My box office team have been wonderful under pressure!" (He might show his exhaustion and pride and sense of self-importance by the way he stands with his chest puffed up, and his voice indicating the strain of the effort.)

The director of the play: "The box office do a great job but they've paid to see my performance! Well, I've done all I can. It's over to the actors now. I'm going to sit back and watch and enjoy!" (The director may show his sense of 'I'm the best' by his voice and the way he stands, as if he is looking down on others.)

An actor: "We couldn't have done it without the director but from now on the eyes of the audience will be on us. Success or failure is in our hands!" (This actor will give a strong impression with voice and body language that 'I'm the centre of the universe you know, everything else is a mere detail'.)

The stage manager: "The audience will be watching and enjoying what goes on, on the stage. What they don't see is the crucial work behind the scenes. What you see can only happen because of what you don't see! I'm the stage manager in charge of all that. It is a vital job! I hardly ever get a mention!" (The stage manager will be annoyed that he doesn't get acknowledged for what he does.)

The costume designer: "Behind the scenes is vital but the beauty of the characters is enhanced by my wonderful costumes! Hundreds of hours of sewing and all over in two hours!" (The costume mistress will have a feeling of great pride.)

The lighting supervisor: "Costumes are marvellous. But never forget that nobody would see anything without the skill of my lighting!" (The person in charge of lighting will also feel great pride.)

The sound editor: "Seeing it is fine but without me nobody would hear a thing. After all, the word 'audience' actually means 'what you hear'." (This person may feel pleasure from a feeling of 'I know more than you do!')

The ice cream vendor: "I've listened to each of you. Does anyone want an ice cream?" (This person may display a feeling that shows an inferiority complex, not realizing what a great job he does.)

EXTENSION IDEA

Ask students to explore other team situations where all the people depend on each other. Present it in a similar way. Here are a few ideas:

o The crew of a fishing ship including captain (skipper), deckhand, chef, navigator.

o The staff of a bank including manager, cashier, messenger, secretary, receptionist.

o A cross section from the army including general, regimental sergeant major, private.

- The staff of a restaurant including manager, chef, waitress, cleaner.
- A hospital including doctors, nurses, matron, cleaners, cooks, surgeons.
- A football team including manager, captain, trainer, coach, doctor.

AIM: To explore conflict situations through role-play and experiment with different severities of conflict and argument.

SETTING THE SCENE

Someone has had a wind turbine put up in his garden. The idea is to generate electricity. The wind is blowing and the owner, who is in the garden, is looking up at it proudly. His point of view is that the turbine has the following advantages:

o It is environmentally friendly
o It is cheaper than normal electricity
o It is the way forward. Soon everyone will have them.

His neighbour, however, is not so keen. In his opinion the turbine has the following disadvantages:

o It blocks out some light
o It's noisy and squeaks at night
o It looks unsightly.

Two students act out a scene in the garden, looking up at the turbine and using the conversation to put both of the above viewpoints.

Ask students to work out another little scene where two opposing viewpoints are verbalized at the scene of the problem. For example:

o A bonfire scene where one person argues that it is an efficient way to get rid of rubbish and the opposing view is that it is air pollution.
o An angling scene in which a fisherman is sitting by the side of a river arguing with a passer-by that it is a relaxing hobby which millions of people enjoy. His antagonist believes that it is wrong and cruel to kill fish for sport.

Experiment with different scenarios and various levels of opposition. This could range from friendly banter through to real anger and annoyance.

AIM: To show the skill of giving the illusion of moving through a strange landscape. Highly imaginative science-fiction-type dangers are experienced along the way.

Students love to allow their minds to run free and create highly imaginative places. Adding danger helps heighten the drama. This activity involves a journey so that they can use their descriptive skills along the way to conjure up images in the mind of the audience. Spontaneity of acting is important here.

Put two chairs together. This becomes a jeep. One student is the driver and the other is the navigator with a map. They are going to drive through strange places, for example:

○ A road that starts off all right and then enters a tunnel and goes deep underground. The tunnel has strange insect-like creatures of all shapes and sizes clinging to its ceiling. Sometimes the tunnel opens up into huge caverns with strange vine-like plants.

○ A mountain road that gets higher and higher. It then gets very narrow and precarious as the jeep gets very close to the edge where there are vast sheer drops to the valleys. Little purple bubble men start to jump out and block their way. If they drive into them they explode like jelly all over the windscreen thus obscuring their view.

○ A road that takes them through a frozen landscape. As they progress, small holes appear in the road and they have to dodge round them. Further into their journey the holes get bigger and ice creatures start to run at them and throw snowballs at them. The snowballs are no ordinary snowballs. They can pierce right through metal and then steam and smoke! The navigator will call out instructions, such as, "Left, right, now along here for a short while then turn left before you get to the river." He will then concentrate on the map, glancing up now and again. The driver becomes increasingly confused as the directions do not seem to match where they actually are. He will try to clarify things with questions like, "Should we go under the bridge?"

Students are good at inventing and improvising landscapes. The realism and illusion is enhanced if the students look around and give the impression of things passing by. Leave a bit of time between each instruction to suggest the movement of the car.

Get them to invent all sorts of landmarks and let them drive through and explore amazing things. While they are doing this create problems for them that will make them incorporate these into their acting. Problems may include things like, "But the desert seems to stretch out in every direction! Which way do we go?" or, "I can't go forward because we're on the edge of a cliff!" As time goes on make the descriptions of what they see more and more strange. For example:

o "There seems to be hot purple bubbly liquid covering the road!"
o "Look at that! It's a massive tree; bright yellow and green spikes are falling from it. Oh no! One has pierced the bonnet!"

When these two students run out of ideas, get the next pair up.

TEACHING STYLES

AIM: To explore different teaching styles during paired work.

For this activity ask students to find a partner. One will be the 'student' and one will be the 'teacher'. The activity will explore a range of styles and methods of teaching and instruction as well as a range of contexts.

First, the teacher has to get the student to carry out an activity using an aggressive bullying approach. It may be a sergeant major shouting at a cadet about how to polish his boots and how awful they are.

The next approach may be in stark contrast with, say, a country vicar teaching a church member about kindness by explaining with a smile and a gentle voice that life's purpose is to love each other.

Then they could try a football coach using an encouraging warm approach to teach a football technique to a player. Contrast this with a manager calling a player 'rubbish'!

Next could be a chef demonstrating how to make a cake but this time the talk is too fast, the instructions are disordered and unclear and the voice mumbles the words.

Try to cover a range of skills and knowledge in a variety of teaching situations. Remind students that teaching happens constantly through situations across the world and not just in a classroom.

The students could then discuss common factors of good teaching, and come up with their own scenarios that demonstrate examples of both good and bad teaching. Ask for volunteers from students who are quite good at something and suggest they teach, and exhibit a variety of teaching styles to their partner.

AIM: To demonstrate that the descriptions of things can be significantly affected by mood and personality.

DEMONSTRATION

Get four students, A, B, C and D to sit back-to-back so that they look out towards the four directions of the compass: north, south, east and west. A particular landscape is suggested to their imaginations, for example, the mountains of Scotland.

Each student is given an emotional viewpoint. For example, A is joyful, B is worried and frightened, C is sensitive to beauty and D is bored.

Each student then looks into the distance and gives a short monologue, in which they imagine and describe in detail what they see in terms of their emotional viewpoint. For example:

A: "Look at those fantastic mountains reaching up into the sky. Doesn't it make you feel great to be alive?"
B: "I see people climbing these mountains in the distance. What if they fell? Imagine the awful pain and anguish!"
C: "The purple heather, the white clouds, the way the sun glints on the granite peaks. It is so beautiful!"
D: "They're just mountains. Mountain after mountain. When you've seen one, you've seen them all. They don't do anything, they just sit there."

DEVELOPMENT

Produce a set of cards describing different types of landscapes, e.g. seascape, desert, jungle and city. Have another set of cards describing different emotional states and moods.

Divide the class into groups of four and ask them to act out a similar situation to the demonstration using a variety of landscapes and moods. Allow some rehearsal time and then each group can perform to the rest of the class.

At the end of each presentation ask the rest of the group to guess what each character's mood was supposed to be.

THE SUPERMARKET OF THE FUTURE

AIM: For students to invent and then act out products of the future that can talk.

The students can be given ten minutes' preparation and experimentation time in small groups. The teacher can provide a set of initial ideas for products and then encourage the students to come up with their own. Students line up to represent a line of products on the shelves of an aisle in the supermarket. In this futuristic shop the shoppers press a button on the product and the product sells itself and gives information. For example:

> I am a new type of baked bean. I'm in a tin but I taste real fresh. Press button B on the tin and ten seconds later I'm on your plate ready cooked.

Encourage students to come up with futuristic ideas about the product, about how it is stored and how it can be cooked. For example:

> Brr, I'm frozen green peas. If you want me to be another colour just select the colour button on the side of my special box and I'll be any colour you want. But I'll still taste great!

Encourage students to make funny voices and sounds to match the product, for example:

> I look like a boring old loaf of bread. But push my button and select which type of bread you want and within 15 seconds I become that mouth-watering product.

Arrange it so that shoppers saunter down the aisles like they do in a supermarket, pressing the buttons of the products here and there. It works well if the information soundtrack is kept short, loud, clear and punchy.

Don't limit it just to food products. The main thing is to let the imagination run wild as to how products will be in the future. Anything is possible.

AIM: To role-play survival activities in the context of a competition.

Split the class into five groups and appoint a team leader for each group. Prepare a list on the board and for each item prepare a card with that item on it. If you are feeling ambitious (and it is well worth the effort) collect props to represent the items. The list should include the following items:

o   emergency food ration box
o   fire lighting flint
o   distress flare
o   mirror
o   plastic sheets
o   first-aid kit
o   water storage bottle
o   water distillery kit
o   compact spade
o   telescope
o   large bar of chocolate
o   silver emergency hypothermia blanket
o   knife
o   string
o   fishing line and hook
o   small animal trap
o   sun hat
o   sun cream
o   compass
o   joke book
o   notebook and pencils
o   bag of spare clothes
o   headache tablets
o   detailed map of the location
o   special lightweight tent
o   torch
o   soap
o   wind-up radio
o   SAS survival handbook
o   sunglasses.

Taking it in turns, each member of the group must select an item for their survival challenge. The teacher will then describe a survival situation. (An example is given below.) The groups then have to work out how they will survive, and use the items they have selected. They will then act out examples of the use of those items. A competition will be set with the teacher as judge to award top marks for the most convincing survival group. Here is a possible survival situation:

You are marooned in a dense jungle area in the depths of the Amazon rainforest. With your group and the items you have managed to collect, explain and act out how you will survive and be rescued. The dangers you face are sweltering heat, a host of dangerous animals and insects, deep fast-flowing rivers to cross and remoteness from any human settlement.

AIM: To dramatically read from a 'talking diary' and describe key events in an experience. The 'journey' can be of any type, for example, an adventure, a relationship or a new job.

Here is an example of a diary recording a planned voyage around the world:

○ "I'm planning to sail around the world in one year's time. Isn't it exciting?"

○ "There are ten months to go and I'm busy trying to get sponsors."

○ "With nine months to go I didn't realize how hard it would be to get sponsors. I've asked over 200 people and only nine have agreed to sponsor me. I've got £10,000 but I need another £50,000! What am I going to do? How embarrassing!"

○ "Fantastic news! With only six months to my sail date a kind businessman has sponsored me for the remaining amount I need. Everything should be good from now on. Main hurdle over!"

○ "I'm getting really nervous now. Four weeks to go! I've checked and double-checked all the plans and bought all the equipment I need. I've gone for the very best quality!"

○ "I sail in three days and last night I had a farewell party with family and friends. It was very emotional. But I must remain positive! It will be an adventure of a lifetime!"

○ "I'm off! I couldn't believe today how many boats came to see me off! I'm high on adrenaline and the wind is behind me. This is fantastic."

○ "Disaster! One week in and a storm like I've never known off the coast of Africa nearly turned my vessel over last night. It was terrifying. Why did I ever do this?"

And so on. Ask the students to think up an experience and write diary notes so that they can be read out dramatically from the 'talking diary'. Here are some more examples of experiences and scenarios that could be explored with the 'talking diary':

○ Key points from a first day at primary school, first day at secondary school, first day at university or first day at a new job.

○ Key points from moving to an old people's home describing what life is like.

○ Key events from one year in an ambulance driver's life.

○ Key events from one year in a film star's life.

○ Key events from an explorer's trip to Mars.

AIM: To act out and show the contrast in living conditions between two families, one on a low income, the other materially well off.

SUMMARY

A family who live cramped up in a caravan act out their experience and compare it with a family who live luxuriously in a mansion.

Arrange two groups of, say, five students at each side of the acting space. Group one is a family who live in a caravan and group two is a family who live in a massive mansion.

The first scene is breakfast. Group one act out eating breakfast cramped around a small table and each movement, such as taking a packet from a cupboard, is awkward and cramped. They keep bumping into each other. Their talk is fast and harassed and stressed. In contrast, family two are spaciously seated around a large table and are served by a butler who moves around the table at a stately pace. The talk is quiet, calm and dignified.

It works well if one group runs a sequence of a few minutes and then freezes the action while the other group acts out and then vice versa, scene by scene.

The next scene could be playing a game. Group one could be cramped around a small table again, this time playing a board game and mention could be made of heavy rain outside while in contrast family two are playing hide and seek around their huge property. Again, run a sequence of action and then freeze it and then run the other family sequence. It works well in the mansion if the talk makes reference to the vastness of the place, for example, "There you are Martha, I've searched the cellars and thought I saw you nip into the billiard room, and here you were hiding in the library!"

Get the students to think up other activities that could take place. Keep the focus on showing the contrast between cramped conditions and lots of space and how this affects attitude and actions.

Stage Craft

ATTACHING MEANING

AIM: To experiment with and explore how our perspective can be changed by background knowledge.

Work out small drama scenes without at first saying what they are or what they mean. This activity will show how we interpret and understand drama differently in accordance with what we already know about what we are seeing. For example, ask two people to walk towards each other and meet in the middle of the acting space and then shake hands. This is done without comment of any kind. The audience wonders who they are and what is happening. Now do it again but this time a narrator introduces the action before it happens with:

> "After years of bitter war the leaders of these two great countries have met for the first time and shaken hands on a peace agreement. A historic day!"

Now do it again but this time the narrator introduces it with:

> "He had waited years for this moment. To meet his hero. At last that day had come!"

Note how what we see changes in our minds. Get students to experiment with different small dramas with narrators introducing and attaching different meanings to see how it changes the way we see the drama.

AUDIENCE REACTION

AIM: To show how what happens on a stage is affected by the audience reaction.

This activity shows that actions and words are changed by the way the audience reacts to them. It underlines the communal essence of drama and theatre.

STEP 1

Ask for a volunteer who steps out in front of the rest of the class. She then tells a simple animated tale of what she did that day, with simple actions. It can be what she actually did do that day, or it can be completely made-up. The first time she does it the audience must be silent.

STEP 2

She tells the animated tale again but this time the audience cheers and claps at the end of each little section. She then does it again with lots of booing and heckling. Yet again the audience could laugh a lot at the tale.

STEP 3

Ask for more volunteers to tell different tales adding as many actions as possible. The rest of the class then react in a variety of ways. There should be actions as well as words to show that reactions from the audience can be powerful in reaction to both. Below are some examples and ideas for the students to work with:

o "This morning I enjoyed a lovely boiled egg." (Hold up two fingers to show size of egg. The audience cheers.)

o "When I got on the bus this morning I started to feel a bit sick. The way the bus was driven I felt worse . . ." (Student staggers about imitating the jerky movements of the bus. Audience laughs out loud.)

o "You'll never guess what my cat caught last night. It was a big bright green frog." (Student cups hands as if holding the frog. Audience reacts with a loud "Urghh . . ." sound.)

○ "I waited at the pictures last night for my friend to turn up. It started to rain and she, she, never arrived." (Student puts his head in his hands. Audience says "Ahhh.")

Discuss with the whole class the powerful effect that the audience has on the drama.

AIM: To show how dramatic interest can be enhanced by building anticipation.

The best way to show the build-up of anticipation is with a comparison exercise. Arrange a group of students, say, five, to adopt the stance and actions of a party in someone's house. They are eating and drinking, happy and having fun. New guests arrive and are greeted with cries of "Hallo!", "How are you?", "May I take your coat?" etc. Names are mentioned, for example, "Hallo Michael, how's Jane getting on?" Someone called Brian Greenaway arrives and mingles in.

Run the scene through again as above but just before Brian Greenaway arrives get the noise to soften and turn the conversation to talk about Brian. Here is an example of the sorts of things that could be said:

A: "Does anybody know when *he's* due to arrive?"

B: "Exciting, isn't it?" (looks at her watch)

C: "Incredible to think that he's been in so many films!"

D: "He is definitely coming, isn't he?"

A: "Definitely."

B: "Will it be all right to take a photograph?"

C: "Wait till he's been here a while."

B: "What about an autograph?"

C: "Let's be careful not to surround him too quickly."

Then Brian arrives. Notice how, this time, the audience's interest in Brian is much enhanced.

Ask the students to work out their own mini-plays where anticipation is built up in some way before the main character arrives.

IDEA 55

AIM: To show emotion through use of facial expression, voice and body language.

Ask a group of five students to form a line facing the audience. The teacher calls out an emotional state and the students adopt a facial expression to show that emotion and hold it for a few moments. They do not move their bodies and no sounds are made at this stage. The emotional state could be fear, love, anger, jealousy, happiness, hate, boredom etc.

The emotions are then called out again, in random order and this time the faces must be blank and expressionless but the body adopts a stance or posture that represents the emotion. For example, the students could show 'confusion' by putting their hands on their heads.

The next step is to run the emotions through with facial expression and posture. Try it again and then add small movements.

The last step is to add a sound or say a few words to reinforce the emotion. Ask the students to form into groups of roughly six. One member of the group should call out different emotions for the others to respond to.

EXTENSION IDEA

Experiment with small role-play activities, for example, preparing breakfast, where one student acts it all out, governed by a particular emotion, with another student who is governed by a different emotion. Remind them to deploy facial expressions, body language, tone of voice and movements to amplify and show that particular state of mind.

AIM: To create a stage set using human sculptures.

Stage sets are created by using people as props. Start with an empty space and then build up a stage set, a bit at a time. Here is a worked example:

Arrange a group with, say, ten in it. One of the group will be the director and has the authority to direct the others. The scene is a ruined castle and it's a set for a horror play.

A couple of students can make the arch-shaped door and flanking each side will be the heavy, thick and strong walls. Outside will be the deep moat and weeping willows will be arranged hanging into the moat. A bridge will cross the moat to the castle door. This set is made entirely from human sculptures.

A good method is to encourage the students to discuss their ideas and share them. Experiment and try out different ideas and then get the director to decide and set up the finished article. It will then be presented to the rest of the group by the director, who may say, for example, "This is the set for a horror play. It is a ruined castle!" The students then get into position and hold still while the director points out what each component represents.

The next group then present their set in a similar way. Here are some ideas for sets:

○ a desert island for a romance play
○ a railway station for a thriller
○ a large boat for an adventure play
○ the interior of a country house for a murder mystery
○ a dining room for a situation comedy.

The students can then think up and present their own ideas.

IDEA 57

DIRECTOR'S INSTRUCTIONS

AIM: To show how the director's instructions have a dramatic effect.

Arrange groups of three students where one plays a customer, one plays a shop assistant and a third directs. Outline the following scene to the class:

> A customer buys a mobile phone and finds it cannot be charged up. She takes it back to the shop the next day and the following conversation takes place between A (the customer) and B (the shop assistant):

> A: "Excuse me, I bought this yesterday but it doesn't seem to charge up."
> B: "Have you got the receipt?"
> A: "Yes, it's here somewhere." (finds and produces the receipt)
> B: "I'm afraid this is a sale item."
> A: "What does that mean?"
> B: "It means we can't change it."
> A: "But it doesn't work."
> B: "So you said."
> A: "Well what can you do about it?"
> B: "Not a lot . . ."

Run the scene through and continue it and then try different versions. Then run it through again with the director requesting changes to see how they alter the dramatic effect. Here are some examples of the sorts of changes that could be requested:

- change tone of voice
- change volume of voice
- change where they stand
- speed up and slow down delivery
- exaggerate body language
- underplay and use minimal body language.

Ask students to work out other little scenario role-plays that can then be run through in different ways in accordance with the director's instructions and suggestions.

AIM: To demonstrate how focus can be shifted on a stage.

This activity is designed to show how you can focus the attention of the audience onto one part of the action in a drama. Arrange for a group of students to act out a short scene. The scene needs to involve input of talk and action from each of the characters in the scene. For example:

Three people are waiting in a takeaway fish and chip shop and two people are serving behind the counter. The people behind the counter are doing normal things like cooking the fish and chips, wrapping them up, chatting and taking the money. The chat is about the weather and football etc. Try to create a typical scene from everyday life. It doesn't matter exactly what the scene is; the important thing is to run through it a few times like a rehearsal until each student knows exactly what to do.

The next stage is to start making the changes. First, run the scene through again but this time nobody speaks except one of the characters. She talks and responds *as if* the others are talking. Then try running the scene again, but this time with everyone frozen except one character who carries on *as if* the others are moving and responding in the normal way.

Notice how the focus of attention is shifted each time. How else could focus be directed and redirected? Ask students to work out their own simple scene and experiment with shifts of focus.

AIM: To make and use a mask to dramatize the 'heart of an object'.

This is a highly creative and surreal activity, which is great fun and simple to prepare. Ask the students to bring in a mask and think about the heart of an object. Ask them to try to get to the essence of what makes an object what it is. Here are some examples of objects and what might be considered their 'hearts':

○ A cactus plant. The heart may be prickles, so a student may have made a simple cardboard mask of a cactus plant and say, "I'm a cactus plant. Nobody likes touching me because I'm so prickly to touch!"

○ A cup of tea. The heart is relaxation and enjoyment, therefore a student may wear a mask of a cup of tea and say, "I'm a lovely hot cup of tea. When people drink me they feel good inside. But be careful, don't spill me or I'll scald you."

○ A dartboard. The heart is darts being thrown at it, so a student wearing a mask of a dartboard may say, "I'm getting fed up with my life. I have hours of silence during the night and most of the day and then, ouch, ouch, ouch . . . they keep throwing little darts at my face and then cheer!"

The mask can be very simple, for example, a cornflakes packet cut into a circle with two eyes. The student could hold the mask in front of his face and describe his life as a cornflake. Encourage them to let their imaginations go. For example:

I love being a cornflake. Here I am crisp and solid and then all that milk sloshes over me (body to sway in response) and then crunch! Crunch! Crunch! I give people energy all morning! It's great being a cornflake!

The next mask comes up. Keep the activity brisk, one after another. Quick-fire for this brings out the best! The next one might be a picture of a camera with two eyes. Keep it simple. Or just hold a camera in front of the face. The student needs to go for the essence of that object's existence. Remember to match the tone of voice to the character of the object. The 'camera mask' might say, "When I'm held up everyone keeps still and smiles at me. I am important!" The student may stand proudly for a few moments and then get off the acting space and the next actor steps up.

Encourage students to come up with their own ideas. Remember, the key is to get to the heart of the object.

AIM: To explore how music can powerfully set a mood to the action of the drama.

Select four different pieces of music that are completely different in mood, for example:

o happy
o sad
o mysterious
o fast moving.

Ask students to get into small groups and think up a one-minute play on the theme of one of the four moods. Act out the scene with actions and words and no music. Then act it out with the words and actions and the appropriate music played quietly in the background. Then act out the scene in mime with the appropriate music quite loud. Then start experimenting with different moods of music set to different one-minute plays. Experience how powerful music is at setting a mood. For example, a scene where a small group are walking slowly along will appear triumphant when Elgar's Pomp and Circumstance is played but the same sequence of action with a slow movement of Mahler will seem intensely sad.

HOW MUSIC ENHANCES DRAMA

AIM: To experiment with minimal scenery to show how it can produce maximum setting effect.

The term 'iceberg' refers to the idea of only a fraction of something being on show while the vast majority is unseen below the surface. In the case of 'iceberg scenery' it is fascinating to experiment with the idea that a few sound effects and minimal bits and pieces of scenery which are seen in an acting area can evoke a vast significance in the imagination of the audience. Sometimes, of course, a play will have a very detailed and extravagant set that would have taken weeks to construct. In this idea, minimal preparation produces maximum creative results.

There will be a bit of preparation required in collecting, or perhaps making, symbolic scenery items and pieces of music etc. and this can be organized as a piece of homework for the students to bring an item in for the following lesson. Here are some examples of how the scene can be effectively set using this idea:

○ Have a table, covered with a plain white sheet, in the acting space with a couple of candlesticks on it. In the centre place a cross. On the screen at the back, project a colour OHT (overhead transparency) of a stained glass window and in the background have some music of monks chanting. Turn off some of the lights and suddenly we have entered the world of the medieval church.

○ Try an empty space with one chair. On the screen project a colour picture of a tree and a soundtrack of birdsong. With as little as this, we enter the world of a garden in summer.

Ask the students to plan ideas of their own so that OHTs and soundtracks can be provided for experimenting in the following lesson. Once these minimalist scenes are created, have fun in acting out little improvised mini-scenes that pick up the atmosphere.

AIM: To explore awareness and use of body tension.

In drama an important element is awareness and control of tension in the body. Try some exercises that explore this.

Imagine that there is a scale of 1 to 10, where 1 is a level of tension where walking is so relaxed that it is almost sleepwalking and 10 is a state of high alert. Ask students to walk around the space slowly and adopt the appropriate level of tension as the teacher calls out different numbers and allows them a few moments to adopt and then move around to that particular level of tension.

The next step is to act out an ordinary scene with the focus on a level of tension. For example, ask a few students to stand in a bus queue and wait patiently with a relaxed level of tension. Then try it with a high level of tension where students are anxiously looking up the road and checking their watches etc.

Ask students to work out their own mini-scenes trying it first with a relaxed feel and then running through again with more tension.

IDEA

62

LEVELS OF TENSION

MIME CARDS

AIM: To practise mime activities with immediate feedback from the rest of the group.

The teacher prepares a set of mime cards. For this to work well the activities need to be very varied and cover a range of difficulties. The cards could also contain a few helpful tips.

The idea is for a student to read the card, think about it and then mime out an activity that the rest of the group have got to guess.

It is important for no one to try to guess until the activity is finished. This is a most important rule. When someone thinks they know what is being mimed they must put up their hand for the teacher to ask them. Here are some examples of mime cards:

EASY MIME CARD

Brushing your teeth: Mime the action of brushing your teeth and glancing in the bathroom mirror.

MEDIUM DIFFICULTY MIME CARD

Waiting for a bus where you are worried about the time.

TIP: Look up and down the road with a worried expression and keep glancing at your watch.

DIFFICULT MIME CARD

Opening a letter and reading bad news.

TIPS: Carefully open the envelope and unfold the letter in a normal mood. Allow time to read the letter and slowly let the words and message sink in. Show by your face that it is bad news. If students can't guess the mime then feed them clues and allow the mimer to mime it through again before you reveal the answer.

AIM: To show how a scene can be set in the imagination of the audience with careful narration creating word pictures.

Here we have some experiments where a scene can be set by using a narrator's short introduction.

SCENE 1

Four students stand in a line, keeping perfectly still and having blank faces. Allow the audience to look at them standing there for a few moments. The narrator then steps on and says:

> "It is nearly midnight." (pause) "The air is frozen." (pause) "Look, the moon is full and casts silver light on the edges of these ancient gravestones in this ancient graveyard." (pause) "It is silent and deathly still." (pause) "Listen, can you hear the rats scurrying in the undergrowth?"

Nobody moves or acts. The students being watched just stand still and the narrator sets the scene with words. By keeping still, the students 'become' (in the mind of the audience) the gravestones by the magic transformation created by the narrator's description of the scene.

SCENE 2

Four students sit on the floor, making themselves as small as possible. The narrator steps out and says:

> "It is mid-afternoon on a hot July day. The sun is blazing down. The farmworkers have been up since dawn, harvesting the hay, and are now a mile away in a pub drinking beer. Look at the fruits of their labours, these bales of hay, left to dry out in the sun, in the corner of this field. Look, see how huge the field is. And beyond the field another field and another stretching out in blazing yellow as far as the eye can see." (pause) "Can you smell the freshly cut hay? Listen, can you hear the bees and the birdsong?"

Ask students to think up their own scenarios where a narrator can bring to life the scene in the imagination of the audience.

AIM: To experiment with scenes set by projected backdrops.

For this idea you will need an overhead projector and a set of OHTs with colour pictures of various locations in the world. For example, you may have a cityscape, a forest scene, a mountain scene, a seascape and a desert. The lights are dimmed and the slide is projected onto the screen, acting as a backdrop and setting the mood.

The students will work in pairs. It helps if copies of the OHTs have been provided in advance for the pairs of students to practise with. They then act out a little scene that involves a journey through the landscape depicted by the backdrop. They don't have to move about much. The journey is referred to by conversation. Here is an example, with the projected backdrop being a jungle scene in which two students, explorers A and B, cut through the air with their long powerful knives. They are wiping the sweat from their brows:

A: "It's no good. We've been hacking our way through this dense jungle for days. We're hardly making any progress."

B: "I'm thirsty and there's hardly any water left."

A: "These soldier ants are crawling all over me." (makes action to frantically brush off the ants)

B: "When did we last eat?"

A: "I think it was yesterday. I'm getting drowsy with this heat and I can't think straight."

B: "We're hopelessly lost. What are we going to do?"

SETTING THE SCENE – WITH PROJECTIONS

THE INTERNAL MONOLOGUE

AIM: To show that what is said can be different from what the character is thinking, achieved by the presentation of private and public thoughts.

For this you set up a situation and act it out but each actor has a 'shadow' actor who stands near the actor and speaks and reveals the 'internal monologue' or private thoughts of the actor. (As a method, the actor speaks as naturally as possible and then after a tiny pause the voice of the shadow actor is heard, before the next actor speaks.) For example:

A is an old person and AA is the shadow actor
B is the old person's son and BB is the shadow actor
C is a care home owner and CC is the shadow actor
D is a resident of the care home and DD is the shadow

THE SCENARIO
The four of them have met at an old people's home. After years of indecision, 'A' has nearly decided to live in a home but is naturally very worried about things.

A: "I will get my own room, won't I?"

AA: "I'm so worried about my privacy."

C: "The best thing to do is to ask my long-term resident here."

CC: "Profits are down this month. I desperately need some more residents."

D: "Yes, you will of course get your own room, don't worry." (smiles at C)

DD: "I'd better not mention the fact that I had to share a room when we got a bit full last year."

B: "Well father, it all seems lovely. What do you think?"

BB: "I'm so stressed out keeping an eye on poor old dad that I desperately need a break."

Ask the students to work out their own little mini-plays using the internal monologue.

AIM: To set the scene in an empty space in the imagination of the audience by using voices.

THE SET UP
Arrange about six students around quite a large empty space. These students will call out dramatic descriptions to bring the place alive, like magic, in the imagination of the audience.

TIP: After a voice calls out a descriptive detail, sometimes allow time for the imagination to 'take it up' and visualize it. Try to keep the wording in the present tense and use words like, "Look over there", "Listen", "Notice".

The teacher could begin and join in to keep the momentum going. It helps to be specific and use fine details. Here is an example:

Teacher: "A railway station on a beautiful early summer's morning."

Student 1: "Sunlight is streaming in."

Student 2: "People are hurrying out of the café with plastic cups, looking up at the train timetables."

Student 3: "Look over there. The woman who sells the flowers has produced a lovely stall. Pinks, and yellow and red roses."

Student 4: "Listen. The loud speaker is blaring: 'The next train at platform 1 leaves for Liverpool Street station at 0700 hours!'"

Student 5: "Notice the platform cat, all skinny and old. It is licking itself in the sunshine, oblivious to the hurry and bustle all around it."

Student 6: "Over there. The ticket collector, walking sprightly and smiling. He loves his job. What is that in his hand? A ticket clipper!"

Student 1: "The screech of brakes from a train a little way off."

Student 2: "The smell of new green paint on those railings . . ."

And so on. Ask the students to create their own 'voices scene' in groups, based on one of the following:

- a lighthouse in a storm
- a cricket match
- an old ruined house
- an airport
- a Spanish beach.

Allow the groups a few minutes to work out a 'scene'. The idea can be enhanced by further preparation. If the teacher has ready a series of descriptive sentences on cards they can help students with ideas. The students could also prepare a few ideas of their own in advance.

Bringing Language and Literature Alive

AIM: To dramatize the poem 'The Rhyme of the Ancient Mariner' by Samuel Taylor Coleridge.

Examples are shown to help stimulate a larger project to dramatize much more of the poem. The process is a 'dramatic commentary'. It requires a narrator to read the selected lines, a commentator to point things out and the audience is used to heighten the drama at certain times.

> *He holds him with his skinny hand,*
> *"There was a ship," quoth he.*

The line is quoted by a narrator and an old man puts up his hand to hold the arm of another man. They then freeze the action and hold still.

The commentator points things out to the audience, e.g., "Look, his hand is skinny from years of hard work on the ships. His voice is mysterious, listen . . ." The line is then repeated as the audience looks at the freeze frame. The next line is quoted:

> *The ship was cheered, the harbour cleared . . .*

This time there are no actors. The commentator walks to the centre of the stage and evokes the imagination of the audience. He may point and say, "Look, the ship has been got ready, full of supplies with all the decks clean and gleaming. The huge white sails have been hoisted up and hundreds of people are at the side of this dock cheering the crew as the ship starts to sail off. Come on, wave and cheer!" The audience is invited to wave and cheer. When the noise fades the following line is quoted:

> *And now the Storm-blast came, and he*
> *Was tyrannous and strong . . .*

A group of actors (say seven) act out the pulling of ropes on a ship that is in a storm. They look up, pull hard on the ropes and then sway from side to side. They then freeze and the commentator walks on.

Commentator: "Come on, let's hear that storm." The audience is invited to make the noise of rain and waves and thunder. The commentator signals for them to stop. He looks at the sailors. "Look, all through history sailors have bravely fought against the raging storms and the huge oceans."

And so on. Pick out key lines of the poem and continue with this method.

EMOTION BEHIND THE WORDS

AIM: To show how the meaning of words can be changed by the voice used.

Take a small extract of poetry. For example:

A thing of beauty is a joy forever
Its loveliness increases, it will never
Pass into nothingness.

Get the students to say the words in different ways. Here are some suggestions:

o say it as if you are very sad
o say it as if you are very joyful
o put emphasis on certain words
o say it as if you are arguing with someone
o say it like a speech to many people
o say it as if you are confused
o say it as if halfway through you get angry
o say it as if you are introducing a guest on a TV chat show
o say it as if you are alone and you are becoming increasingly scared.

Prepare a variety of short poetry extracts on cards and get students to experiment with saying them over and over in different ways using some suggestions from above and inventing more of their own.

Remember to make other variations. For example, alter the volume and speed and try standing still and then try moving about.

The experience will reveal how meanings can be changed endlessly by delivery. The words themselves do not contain the ultimate meaning but can be changed in a huge variety of ways.

AIM: To dramatically perform a Shakespearean sonnet.

Read through with the class sonnet number 27 which begins 'Weary with toil, I haste me to my bed' and explain that in summary the poet is in love with someone and when he goes to bed he continues to think of his love. He is obsessed.

Some key lines will be acted out and then put together in a sequence. A good method is to experiment with mimed movements and then run the movements with the line being simultaneously recited.

Line 1 (above) could be a student crawling across the floor, extremely tired but as quickly as possible, and then lying down in a comfortable bed.

'And then begins a journey in my head' could be several students representing movement around him while he's lying there, for example, mimed swimming, walking etc. and then they fade off.

'For then my thoughts (from far where I abide)/ Intend a zealous pilgrimage to thee' could be shown by a queue of people lined up in front of another student (to represent the object of his love) who, when they get to her, kneel down like pilgrims, pause a moment and then move off so that the next person can kneel in reverence.

'Which like a jewel (hung in ghastly night)/ Makes black night beauteous and her old face new' could be a student standing proud and smiling while a group of students surround her, with hands raised in twisted shapes and frowning faces and then slowly fade away to reveal her standing there, smiling.

The next step is to have someone read the whole sonnet while the key lines are enacted in a smooth sequence.

EXTENSION IDEA

Give small groups of students other sonnets and get them to try to enact them.

ENACTING THE SIMILE

AIM: To enact a variety of similes.

The teacher calls out a list of similes and the students act them out. Allow a few moments for each one. Here are some examples that have produced great responses:

○ walk like a rat
○ walk like a hungry rat
○ walk like a tired cat
○ stand still like a fishing line
○ become a flower with lots of petals
○ become like a bee
○ move like a lawnmower
○ be like a fish landed on the side of the river bank
○ smile like a clown
○ walk like a footballer, walking out at the start of a cup final, in front of a huge crowd
○ salute like a soldier
○ move your arms like a windmill
○ move your arms as if they are hands on a clock face
○ sit like a garden ornament
○ become a seagull
○ move as if you are washing a car
○ walk like a pigeon being chased by a cat
○ creep up on something as if you were a lion hunting
○ look at something as if it was horrible
○ look at something as if it was beautiful.

If there's time get the students to think of some similes themselves which the rest of the class can act out.

AIM: To explore the meanings of clichés through drama.

In these activities students enact clichés in imaginative ways and create tiny mini-plays from them in order to explore their meanings. For example, to enact the cliché 'he was beside himself', two students could stand, one behind the other, and then one student could say in a clear voice, "He was beside himself." The other student could then step out smoothly from behind him and the two would then stand still, just looking at each other.

To enact the cliché 'beggars can't be choosers', the words could be spoken by one student and then another student could act out standing at the side of the road with her hand out, begging. A third student could play a passer-by, stopping to offer some money. The beggar could give the money back while pointing eagerly at the person's watch. Another student could play a police officer who steps up imposingly and says, "Sorry madam, didn't you know that beggars can't be choosers?"

To enact the cliché 'this is breaking the ice nicely', a few students could gather together and stand looking at each other in a nervous, awkward manner. Another student, separate from the group, could swing an axe and say, "This is breaking the ice nicely." The group could then start chatting and being friendly to each other. The narrator could say, "They have broken the ice with each other."

To enact the cliché, 'from the bottom of my heart', a student could play the part of a young man who is looking lovingly at a young lady. In front of them a small group could form the shape of a heart. The young man could then walk slowly around to the bottom of the heart and say, "From the bottom of my heart, I love you!"

There are endless possibilities. Give the students a few clichés for them to go away with and come up with their own ideas and then enact them. Here are a few to be going on with:

FUN WITH CLICHÉS

- ○ 'Don't lead me up the garden path!'
- ○ 'This goes against the grain.'
- ○ 'She led a hand to mouth existence.'
- ○ 'It'll all come out in the wash.'

AIM: To bring out the core meanings of well-known sayings through acting out role-plays.

Collect together well-known sayings and get the students to act them out producing an explanation at the end. It works best in pairs. Here are some examples with ideas of how they could be acted out.

SCENE 1: DON'T CRY OVER SPILT MILK

Two people, A and B, are seated at a table. A accidentally knocks over a bottle of milk. B reacts and starts crying.

A: "Wait a moment, wait a moment. Stop crying straight away!"

B (looking confused): "Why?"

A: "Because you must not cry over spilt milk."

B: "Why not?"

A: "Because what is past is gone and crying won't change it."

B: "OK. Better clear it up and get some more then."

A: "You've got it!"

SCENE 2: NOTHING VENTURED, NOTHING GAINED

Two people are by a phone.

A: "I don't think I will phone up for that job."

B: "Why not?"

A: "Because I've been thinking. I haven't got the experience. I won't stand a chance."

B: "You must try. Nothing ventured, nothing gained."

A: "What do you mean by that?"

B: "If you try, you might get the job. But if you don't try you'll never get the job."

A: "Pass me that phone."

SCENE 3: LOOK BEFORE YOU LEAP

A conversation between two people.

A: "I'm going to sign that contract for that football job."

B: "Have you read it?"

A: "No, but I'm keen to get started."

B: "Look before you leap!"

A: "What do you mean by that?"

B: "Read it carefully so that you know exactly what you're letting yourself in for."

A (reads . . .): "Oh, I see what you mean."

B: "What?"

A: "It says that 50 per cent of my lifetime earnings as a footballer go to my agent."

B: "You see, look before you leap!"

AIM: To give a dramatic performance of someone important to the student.

This activity requires the students to research their hero. This could be a film star, a sports personality, a great person in history or someone they know. They then give a dramatic presentation in which their voices and gestures, body language and attitudes convey the reasons why that person is so important to them. For example:

"My hero is my big brother." (pause, then look up as if looking at someone tall) "When I was young he joined the army." (stand to attention) "He looked so smart in his uniform. He won 'best new recruit' and he was so proud of his award." (stand as if watching him with a proud expression) "He made loads of friends." (act out shaking hands and smiling at people) "He travelled all over the world." (point in slow motion to different directions) "He helped people and did jobs that no one else would do, like collecting rubbish when the dustmen were on strike." (hold nose and look at a huge pile of imaginary rubbish then start throwing it into the cart) "Like putting out fires when the firemen were on strike." (hold a hose and point it at a burning building trying to indicate the heat) "Like driving an ambulance when the ambulance men were on strike." (act out driving, looking tense, and then stand to attention, looking proud) "Yes, I'm proud of my brother."

When one presentation has been made, call up the next student.

AIM: To unlock the magic sound of poetry through dramatic use of voice.

Set up a market with tables and market pitchers and traders. Start with the traders calling out standard phrases that are typically heard at the market, for example:

"Lovely ripe cherries! Who wants them?"

"Best towels in town! Every colour! Every shape! Don't walk by!"

"Gather round! Ladies' watches. Come on men put a smile on their faces!"

"Roll up! Roll up! The last of yer strawberries."

Build up the atmosphere and sound of the market place. Make sure that the phrases are repeated, over and over! Now start to introduce lines from poetry in the same voice as the market-trader phrases. Shout them out. Here are some examples:

"Shall I compare thee to a summer's day?"

"Tread softly, because you tread on my dreams."

"Into the valley of death rode the six hundred."

"Woman much missed, how you call to me, call to me!"

"A thing of beauty is a joy forever."

"Ten thousand saw I at a glance, nodding theirs in sprightly dance!"

"Tiger, tiger, burning bright, in the forests of the night!"

The repeating of the lines unlocks the magic of the sounds of the poetry.

AIM: To produce a rehearsal workshop-type activity to unravel a short scene from one of Shakespeare's plays and highlight the images.

Explain to the class that in this activity a short extract from *Romeo and Juliet* will be looked at very closely and experimented with in order to understand what is happening. Shakespeare's verse is rich in imagery and these images can be 'seen' when sensitively acted out.

ACT 1 SCENE 1: LINES 210 TO 214

She will not stay the siege of loving terms
Nor bide th'encounter of assailing eyes
Nor ope her lap to saint-seducing gold;
O she is rich in beauty, only poor
That when she dies, with beauty dies her store.

Romeo is lovesick for Rosaline, before he meets Juliet, and is telling his friend Benvolio that whatever he does she ignores him. He is very upset by this. Try acting out this small extract. Ask a girl to stand at one end of the acting area and a group of boys at the other. A narrator reads the first line. The boys move with arms outstretched, as if fired from a catapult, one after the other, towards Rosaline as if she is a castle. Just before they reach her, she gently raises her hand and they melt to the floor and lie down. After this happens about five times, there is silence and the line is repeated while they lie there.

Now surround Rosaline with a circle of boys who look admiringly at her and stare.

The second line is read and repeated and one by one the boys lower their heads.

Rosaline now sits and the boys form a queue as if holding precious gold and one after the other slowly load her lap with the gold while the third line is read and repeated. There is then a silence and Rosaline lifts the gold and casts it to one side.

The boys then surround her in a circle and the fourth line is read after which Rosaline lies on the floor and the fifth line is read. Then all the boys lie, as if dead, on the floor and the whole extract is read through.

AIM: To bring a great poem alive and make it fresh in meaning by the use of highly creative dramatization.

Obtain a copy of the poem 'The Tiger' by William Blake. The dramatization will involve the whole class. First, ask six students to mould a giant human sculpture of the face of a tiger. (It would be helpful to have a picture of a tiger's face for reference here. The main thing is to check that it is symmetrical.) Hold the position. It doesn't matter if it looks a bit abstract.

STANZA 1

Pick a chorus. This will be six students who will chant the line 'Tiger, tiger, burning bright' in unison and repeat this line three times as the sculpture holds its pose.

Three students then move in on each side of the 'face' and become trees of the forest. (They may, for example, drape their arms like branches.) The chorus now chants 'In the forests of the night' three times.

A student then walks slowly towards the whole picture and tries to frame it with his hands as an artist might. He then holds a pose (with his hands still framing) to the sound of the chorus chanting 'What immortal hand or eye/ Could frame thy fearful symmetry?'

STANZA 2

'In what distant deeps or skies' could be brought to life by the whole cast pointing into the distance.

STANZA 3

'And what shoulder and what art/ Could twist the sinews of thy heart?' could be brought to life by a set of people making something in a twisting motion with great strain, both mentally and physically. They are creating a heart that will belong to a tiger! What an incredible vision!

Continue to pull out key lines and sculpt images to match. The last stanza is a repeat of the first.

Once everyone has practised their positions and, importantly, moved from one line to another smoothly, run the whole thing through to the chant of the chorus. It will be an impressive sight!

Media

CRIME TV – SOLVED BY YOU

AIM: To act out a reconstruction of a crime in the style of a TV programme.

Select a group of students to act out the scene below. You will need:

○ one TV presenter
○ four family members
○ one police sergeant.

TV Presenter: "Hallo and welcome to *Crime TV – Solved by You*. That's right, you the viewer! This week we've reconstructed, with the help of actors, how you have stumbled upon that vital clue which gave the police that all-important breakthrough. First tonight, the case of the picnic and the binoculars."

SCENE 1

A family group are having a picnic and the students act out setting the picnic things on the blanket. It is a hot day. The presenter's voice-over is heard:

"The Parker family were enjoying a picnic last August in a beautiful part of the countryside. Mr Parker was scanning some distant trees with his binoculars, looking for unusual birds when suddenly . . ."

Show Mr Parker staring through his binoculars with interest and saying things like, "Hallo, hallo, what have we here?" He tells his family that they must immediately drive over to those distant woods despite their protests. "I've seen a group of men bury something deep in the ground in those woods and it looks mighty suspicious."

Show the scene where the Parker family track down the actual spot of disturbed ground. Mr Parker starts digging up the covered-over hole. The voice-over continues:

"It took Mr Parker a whole hour to uncover a black tin box, freshly buried. He never forgot what he found in the box!" (Pause to keep the viewers guessing.)

Switch the scene to the police station where the sergeant congratulates the Parker family. In the box was £100,000 in cash from a recent bank robbery. Clues in the box have now led to the arrest and conviction of the gang.

Ask the class to get into groups and to think up their own crime scenes. They should then act out their own reconstructions to be presented in the style of a TV programme.

AIM: To act out an interview to provide material for a front page story.

Tell the story below to your class:

Claire started up a business that sells computers and which is doing very well indeed. She employs over 100 staff and at the age of 25 she becomes a millionaire. She sets off on holiday, alone, to Hawaii but the plane encounters difficulties over mid-ocean. The plane has to make an emergency landing and all crew and passengers are rescued by a nearby fishing ship. (There are 49 people in all.) All, that is, except Claire. She is missing without a trace. A year later she is legally presumed dead. An amazing thing happens. Ten years later she turns up in London at the offices of her company called Budget Computers, alive and well. All the major newspapers fight over an interview with her to find out what had happened.

Ask students to work in pairs to discuss ideas that might possibly explain her disappearance. Once they have decided, they should work out a sketch to demonstrate her interview with the press. A worked example of the interview follows, in which A represents the reporter and B represents Claire, and the resulting headline is 'Missing Millionaire Riddle: Paradise Island Was Her Saviour. Exclusive!'

A: "Thank you for agreeing to this interview. Everyone is anxious to know what happened."

B: "I'm sure they are."

A: "Well, would you be able to tell us?"

B: "I'd love to."

A: "Well, what did happen to you during those missing ten years?"

B: "When the plane crashed into the sea my life jacket inflated but I became separated from the main group of survivors. After several hours I saw the fishing boat picking up the survivors and I screamed and screamed but it was no good. They sailed off without me! I was terrified and thought that that was it. I was going to die. After many hours I must have fallen unconscious and the next I knew I was lying on a beach with the sun beating down on me. Looking over me was Edgar."

A: "Who is Edgar?" (amazed)

B: "The man who rescued me. He lives on an island."

A: "My goodness. That's incredible." (long pause) "But why was it ten years before you got back to civilization?"

B: "That's a good question. At first I just wanted to get home. Edgar, who owns the island and lives on it alone explained that a supply ship visited his island every month but it had made its last visit only one week ago. When I got into the routine of life on the island it began to dawn on me how stressful and mad my life had been. I did a lot of quiet thinking on that island. It occurred to me that although I was a millionaire that meant nothing when I was alone in that huge ocean. I suddenly realized that money meant absolutely nothing! So I decided to stay on the island. Weeks turned into months. Months turned into years. I became very relaxed and happy. Edgar became a great friend."

A: "This is fascinating. What made you want to come home?" (and so on . . .)

IDEA

80

HIGH ENERGY TV ADVERT

AIM: To act out a TV advert in an appropriate style using a suitable speech register.

Divide the class into pairs and get them to create a product that would change their lives for the better. Then get them to experiment with testimonial type adverts that explain with heightened enthusiasm how this product or service changed their lives. Remind them that the adverts should be short, they should smile a lot while presenting them and they should use very enthusiastic language and presentation.

Once they are all prepared, have them perform the adverts to the class, with one student describing the product and the other acting as the voice-over. It works well if you can get each pair to present their adverts very quickly one after the other as this adds to the fast tempo. For example:

"I used to have a terrible memory. I couldn't remember names or faces! Then I found 'Remember-me-Pills'! After just one week I now have a perfect memory! I'm passing exams, remembering everyone I see! It's fantastic! It changed my whole life!" (huge smile)

Voice-over: "'Remember-me-Pills'. You'll remember their name and never forget anything ever again!"

Or:

"I was so useless at art that people laughed at my efforts. I had no confidence to draw anything. Then I heard about 'Van Gogh Spectacular Spectacles'. I bought a pair and when I wear them I become a great artist! It's true! I've exhibited my art and they're selling for thousands! This is all because of 'Van Gogh Spectacular Spectacles'!"

Voice-over: "'Van Gogh Spectacular Spectacles'. Turn yourself into a great artist today!"

AIM: **AIM:** To develop imaginative descriptions and appropriate styles of presentation.

This activity allows a wide range of students to talk with confidence and detailed knowledge about their toys in an interesting context. (Students feel very confident when describing their own toys. They are authorities on the subject!) They also have to make an imaginative leap and visualize what it would be like to be in the future, looking back. They not only have to describe their toy but make allowances for how it may have aged. In addition to this they present the information in the style of a TV presentation. It is great fun.

Ask students to think of the best toy they've ever had. Allow a few moments for them to visualize it in their minds and then mime as they play with it. Ask them to put it on the floor and just look at it.

Now imagine 50 years go by. There is a special TV programme called *Looking Back At My Toys*.

The teacher sits on a chair with a table between him and another seat. Students are invited up to place their 'toy' on the table, take a seat and talk about it. The teacher is the presenter and gives an upbeat introduction along the lines of, "Welcome to *Looking Back At My Toys*, a new weekly programme where you, the viewer, will bring us your treasured toys from childhood and tell us all about them. Please welcome our first guest today . . ."

The first student speaks about the toy, remembering that he is looking back over 50 years. Here is an example of what he might say:

"As you can see, this is a little teddy bear. It's a bit scruffy now but I've looked after him all these years. His name is 'Jingles' and if you shake him" (mimes shaking the teddy) "you can hear little bells jingling. The bells are in his ears!"

Encourage the students to be active with the toy, picking it up, putting it down and pointing out things and describing it.

IDEA

81

NEW TV PROGRAMME

After a short while the presenter thanks her and calls up the next guest.

AIM: To use a different range of voices to good effect in the production of a radio-style advert.

Arrange the class into groups of four. In the groups they should think up a problem and then decide on a product that will provide a solution. They should then develop an advert suitable for use on the radio making sure that everyone in the group has a chance to speak. Try a structure like the one illustrated below:

○ Voice 1 states the problem.
○ Voice 2 increases the problem (elaborates and develops it).
○ Voice 3 introduces the new product and sells it.
○ The whole group make the sounds of enjoying the product.
○ Voice 4 speaks the powerful tag line.
○ Voice 1: "Kids! Are you fed up with all those monotonous computer games? Do they all seem the same? Do they cut you off from your friends? Are you in your own little world when you play them?"
○ Voice 2: "Would you like to sit and enjoy the company of your friends and play a good old traditional board game?"
○ Voice 3: "A board game, that is, which is traditional in form but bang up to date in content? Well why not buy the new 'Detective Case Box' available in all good toy shops now?"
○ Whole group: make the sounds of people playing the game and having great fun.
○ Voice 4: "The new 'Detective Case Box' – play games without losing the company of your friends!"

129

IDEA

83

AIM: To work in a group as part of a production team to develop a new product and then to present a TV advert in an appropriate style.

These work best if you have groups of around four or five students. This act is divided into two halves. In the first, a scene is acted out in which a problem is encountered. The weight of the problem is emphasized by low heavy voices and heavy moments. Another student should provide a voice-over that asks the viewers if they have ever had that particular problem. Then they should allow a moment to pause. The second half of the advert provides the solution. The students should present this half in an upbeat way, with upbeat voices and actions directly contrasting with the first half. It works well if they end the act with a catchy tag line! For example:

> A student pretends to be an elderly person kneeling down in the garden weeding. The actions are slow and painful. As the student gets up she shows pain in her knees. The voice-over then says, "Finding that kneeling in the garden is a little bit too painful these days? – Well don't worry! The new EXTEND-A-FORK is here!"

The student then pretends to use this wonderful new invention to weed in a standing position. Her movements become light and cheerful. There is a smile on her face. As she goes through a new sequence of movements, demonstrating the wonderful product, the voice-over continues with happy upbeat benefits. For example, "Available in a whole range of colours. The product is fully adjustable and made from special lightweight steel with a lifetime guarantee. Available from all leading DIY shops: EXTEND-A-FORK, because your knees deserve a rest."

AIM: To create and develop portrayals of extraordinary characters and their lives.

Set up two chairs facing each other at an angle and have the class sit in front of these chairs as if they were the TV audience. Guests are to be invited onto this TV chat show where the host (the teacher to start with) will ask them about their extraordinary lives. Here are some ideas for the guests:

○ "I secretly won the lottery jackpot and have given it all away."
○ "I can compose music as good as Beethoven's."
○ "I've got over a thousand photographs with myself and a different famous person."
○ "I was wrongly accused of a crime in a foreign country."
○ "I had a dream and it came true."

Alternatively ask students to think up their own imagined extraordinary lives. Then, as host, ask a student to come up and be interviewed in character. Keep the atmosphere chatty like a TV chat show and the rest of the class will react to what is being said like a live studio audience.

When one guest runs out of things to say, get the next guest on and after the momentum has got going another student might wish to take over as host.

THE EXTRAORDINARY LIFE CHAT SHOW

AIM: To learn to create a mini-documentary from a mythical sighting.

Arrange your class into a circle and discuss with them the mystery of the Loch Ness monster (you may want them to do some research before the class). Then imagine with them that there has been a recent sighting. You'll need:

○ a witness
○ an interviewer
○ a monk
○ a camera operator
○ a narrator
○ a group of students acting together to form the monster.

For example, the witness might say something like this:

"It was a foggy night last night and I was walking back from the pub. I heard a noise at first, a sort of splashing sound coming from the loch. When I looked I saw a blurred dark shape that seemed to rise out of the loch. I moved in closer and couldn't believe what I saw. It was the monster right enough."

The interviewer could then look at the camera and explain that the programme has arranged a history of the Loch Ness monster. This could be acted out as follows:

SCENE 1

Narrator: "It was hundreds of years ago when the monster was first seen. A monk was making his way home to the monastery one night."

Cut to a scene of the monk walking slowly and thoughtfully along, glancing at the loch occasionally.

Narrator: "Suddenly out of the loch loomed a huge beast that towered above the monk."

A group of students can mould together to produce an impression of the monster looming out of the loch. They may wish to move together slowly as a mass and then hold up their arms to give an impression of height.

The students can then show and enact other reported sightings of the monster throughout history with a presenter giving a documentary-style voice-over. At the end the action could return to the present sighting and the presenter can sum up for the news item.

AIM: To develop presentation skills.

Students use their experiences of news programmes to create short 'live' stories, reporting from the street back to the studio. To start with you'll need:

○ 1 presenter
○ 1 reporter
○ 4 witnesses.

Here are some ideas for news items to report on:

○ accidents
○ famous people visits
○ unusual stories
○ scientific discoveries
○ sporting events
○ a factory closing down with subsequent loss of jobs.

Here is a worked example:

Presenter: "Shock news today as we learn of the closure of the IMT factory in North London with the loss of 1,000 jobs. We're going to take you over to our reporter who is at the factory now."

Reporter: "I've been speaking to a lot of the employees today who are clearly shocked and upset. This is Ben Rutkin. He's been working here for 29 years. Ben, when did you hear the news and how do you feel?"

Ben: "I got to work as normal this morning and was handed this." (holds up a sheet of paper) "Next week I won't have a job! I've been here most of my life. I'm devastated. How am I going to pay my mortgage? I've got kids at home!"

Reporter (looking at camera): "I spoke earlier to Sir Norman St Stephens, the managing director. 'Sir Norman, I'm John Watkins from TV News. Why are you closing the factory?'"

Sir Norman: "Look here," (annoyed) "It's not me closing the factory. The bank have called their loan in and we

can't continue trading. I'm sorry for those loyal
workers who have lost their jobs."

Ask the students to work out and present their own
news report based on the format above and then present
it to the rest of the class.

WHAT'S YOUR PASSION? TV COMPETITION

AIM: For students to present something they are interested in, in the style of a high-energy TV competition show, using voice and body language to express enthusiasm.

This activity will require a bit of preparation and so it works best if you set it as a piece of research ready for the next lesson. Ask the students to decide on something that particularly interests them and to research some interesting facts about this topic. They should then practise presenting this research in a colourful, interesting and upbeat way so that they are ready to present it on the new mock TV competition called *What's Your Passion?*

To start with I would recommend that you present the programme, for example:

Presenter: "Hallo and welcome to the new programme, *What's Your Passion?*, in which contestants from all over the nation have just two minutes to share their passion with you, the viewer.

"The best presenter tonight will go on to the finals to be held later this year. At the end of the programme please vote on our special phone-in numbers. So let's sit back and enjoy our first contestant from London who is going to share his passion on birds."

Contestant: "Hi everyone. I'm here today to tell you about birds. What would the world be like without birds? Pretty horrible, eh? Have you ever stopped to think how much we take them all for granted? . . ." (and so on)

The contestant has just two minutes to interest the audience in the subject by the way he talks and presents his research.

It can work well (depending on the group) if a panel of judges give their opinion on each presentation after it has been made.

AIM: To show how fortunes and power relationships can change with the passage of time.

For the initial part of the activity you will need five students to act out the following scene in which N is the narrator, J is Jon, K is Jon's girlfriend Kelly, D is Darren and A is the assistant at the newsagents.

N: "At school Darren is making life hell for Jon. Every time they meet Darren pushes Jon around and makes fun of him." (Act out a short scene where one student pushes another around.)

D: "You'd better keep away from my girlfriend! Or else!"

J: "But Kelly is my girlfriend."

D: "Not any more." (Grabs Kelly's arm and leads her off. Kelly looks shocked and upset.)

N: "Later Kelly and Jon are alone."

K: "I managed to get rid of that creep."

J: "I don't know what to do about him. He's so strong and I'm so weak. He's making my life hell. Every time we meet he bullies me. What should I do?"

K: "Be patient. That's all you can do. You'll see . . ."

N: "Years pass. The two lead very different lives. Jon, who is now 30, eats sensibly, keeps away from drink and cigarettes and works out in a gym three nights a week. He does well in business too. He starts a newsagents and ends up with a whole chain of them. He drives around in a posh car. His body has become strong, lean and powerful. Also, he has become a karate instructor. To top it all he is happily married to Kelly and they live in a wonderful house.

"Meanwhile Darren has not done so well. He eats too much, smokes, and becomes lazy and out of work. He becomes very fat and out of condition. His attitude is very negative about the world. He still tries to bully people but, now 33 and fat and out of condition, nobody is wary of him anymore.

"One day, desperate for work, Darren applies for a
job at one of Jon's newsagents. He hasn't seen Jon for
ten years and has no idea that Jon is the big boss!"

A: "Just a moment sir. I shall just get the manager who
will interview you for the job."
D: (thinks – I'm desperate for this job!)
J: "Hallo, how are you?" (offers his hand, begins to
recognize him . . .)
D: "Hallo, don't I know you from somewhere?" (looks at
him in growing disbelief)

Now divide the class into groups to devise their own
play that continues the story of Jon, Kelly and Darren.
Allow them to choose whether Jon gets revenge or
whether he shows a forgiving and compassionate heart.

THE LANGUAGE OF PERSUASION

AIM: To explore the language (spoken and body language) of persuasion.

You'll need two students to act out the following:

SCENE 1

A student plays a door-to-door salesperson who is trying to get donations for an animal charity. In the following scene, A represents the salesperson and B represents the householder. Useful props would be a clipboard and an identity card for A. The salesperson knocks on B's door. B comes to the door looking harassed (in the middle of cooking something) and the following conversation takes place:

A: "Good afternoon madam, how are you on this beautiful day?"

B: "OK. What can I do for you? I'm extremely busy!"

A: "Could you spare just a few moments now, madam, or would it be more convenient for me to call back later?"

B: "Oh, do it now. But make it quick. As I said, I'm busy."

A: "You look like the sort of person who cares for and loves animals."

B: "Why do you say that?" (suspiciously)

A (looking over her shoulder): "Well, I can see a rather well-fed cat contentedly licking its lips in your hallway!"

B: "Yes, that's Spotty – she don't go short. Who are you anyway?"

A: "May I introduce myself? My name is Robbie and I'm from the National Look After Animals Charity, known as the NLAAC." (shows the identity card)

B: "I see. What do you want? If it's money yer after I ain't got none! We're skint this month!"

A: "Well, it's amazing what even a small donation can do for our specially-built animal sanctuaries. Look, aren't they good?" (shows picture to B)

B (peers at it): "How much?"

Divide the class into pairs and ask them to work out little scenarios where one person has to persuade another person to do something or part with some money.
Practise the scenarios and then show them to the group.

Ideas for Mini-Plays

AIM: To give the students the opportunity to experiment with a particular style of comic theatre.

Divide the class into groups and ask them to have a go at acting out a farce. Remind them that the drama is heightened and very tense and fast moving and 'larger than life'. There are plenty of panic moments!

SETTING THE SCENE

Peter is Jane's brother and they are both teenagers. Their parents have gone to visit someone and have left them in charge of the house overnight. The kids have secretly arranged a party and have invited 20 friends around. The friends are all in the lounge partying. Mrs Kemp is a nosey neighbour. There is a knock at the front door. Peter tries to quieten the noise down and answers it.

Peter: "Hallo Mrs Kemp, how are you?" (door half open)

Mrs Kemp: "I'm very well dear. I thought I'd just pop in to see if you're managing all right without your parents being here." (bending her head around to try to look in)

Peter: "We're absolutely fine, thanks . . ." (trying to push the door to)

Mrs Kemp: "Are you sure? Have you got some visitors?" (bending her head even further)

Peter: "Honestly Mrs Kemp, we're fine and we're going to bed soon for a nice early night! Goodnight!" (shutting the door; Jane appears, looking anxious)

Jane: "Who was that?"

Peter: "Mrs Kemp, checking we're OK."

Jane: "Nosey old bat. Come on, let's enjoy the party while we can . . ." (phone rings)

Jane (answering the phone): "Oh Hi Mum! Yes, we're fine. No, no problems. Pardon? What? The music, oh that's just Pete playing his stuff. No, of course we're not having a party . . ." (A girl rushes out of the party room and shouts at Jane.)

Girl: "Thanks for inviting us Jane . . . it's great . . . there's loads of fit boys here . . ."

Jane (continuing phone call): "Oh, no mum that's just em . . . Peter putting on a silly voice and playing a joke . . . of course we're not having a party . . . yes, love you . . . see you tomorrow . . . yes I won't forget to feed the cat . . ." (rings off)

The students can run through this a few times to get the timing brisk and then discuss ideas (led by the teacher) about other things that can happen in a farce. Remember that a farce is designed to excite laughter by having improbable situations occur, one after the other, in quick succession. In the above case the following may be considered: the neighbour calling again and threatening to phone the police because of the noise; one of Jane's friends accidentally locking herself in a cupboard. Just as Jane is about to unlock the cupboard their parents return home because they have forgotten something. Try to include typical lines like, "What are we going to do now?"; "She'll be here any minute!"; "Oh no! Who's that at the door?"; "Oh, hide in there for a moment, nobody will go in there . . ."

RADIO PLAY CALLED *THE REUNION*

AIM: To act out a love story in a radio play.

SUMMARY

A love story in a radio play is produced making good use of sound effects. This play can be acted out behind a screen so that the audience can hear but not see it, or it can be recorded onto an audio tape and then played back to the audience. A terrific help here is to use a 'sound effects' CD. Here is a worked example:

Narrator: "We join Mabel who is sitting by a computer with her young neighbour."

Mabel (sound of computer keys being pressed): "Thanks for doing this Brian. I really do think it is a hopeless case after so many years."

Brian: "I'm happy to help. This new search engine will find anyone, wherever they are. Now look . . . there is a Malcolm Ray Stephens. Look, there's his phone number. He's in America . . ."

Narrator (low romantic music playing in the background): "Mabel looked with tears in her eyes at the name of the man she fell in love with in the war; the man whose deep blue eyes were still unforgettable; the man who flew off with the United States Air Force and was taken prisoner. A letter was received . . ."

Malcolm (sound of paper being opened. Malcom reads with a strong American accent, Glenn Miller music playing in the background . . .): "My dearest, darling Mabel, don't worry. I was shot down over France and I've got a few injuries, but I'll live. This prison camp isn't that bad. As soon as I'm out of here I will marry you, my darling."

Narrator: "Then the letters stopped. Years went by and no news. Mabel had long considered him dead, but now, 60 years on, with computer technology . . ."

Mabel (sound of a phone ringing): "Is that you, Malcolm? It's me, Mabel." (pause) "Mabel Mackaskill, you must remember me, you were going

to marry me when the war finished . . ." (pause)
"Now don't cry . . ."

Narrator: "And the conversation goes on and on . . ." (a
sound effect to represent time passing, e.g. the loud
ticking of a clock)

Mabel: "This is unreal. He does remember me."

Brian: "Why didn't he contact you?"

Mabel: "Because he lost his memory and when it
returned years later he thought I would be married
with kids and everything. But guess what Brian, he
wants me to fly over to see him. He wants to ask me
something . . ." (stirring closing emotional music)

Ask students to create and act out their own radio
play.

AIM: To act out and continue a play where tension runs high.

Darren is taking his friend Duncan to a traditional travelling fairground. Other students take the parts of fairground traders calling out as follows for business:

○ "Coconuts, knock any one off and it's yours! Come on sir, try your luck."
○ "Gypsy Roselea, I'll read your palm and tell you your future!"
○ "Rifle range, shoot the moving ducks."
○ "Three darts anywhere on the target and you win a prize!"
○ "Correct weight, try your weight!"
○ "Don't be shy, don't walk by – portrait painting!"

Establish an atmosphere of a fair with the two boys wandering around and trying out different stalls, laughing and joking and having fun. Darren notices something on the ground. He picks it up and puts it in his pocket.

A little later they sit down for a drink at a table near a mobile café. Darren carefully takes out his find. It is a wallet and contains a great deal of cash but more importantly a note that gives plans of a crime to be committed that very day at that very place. (In fact, in one hour.) The note could say:

Here's the grand as promised Ed. Now remember, 2 o'clock, Saturday the 14th August, O'Reilly's Travelling Fairground on the meadow north of Cranberry. You know the owner Tom O'Reilly has got a huge stash of cash and jewellery in his caravan hidden in the cereal packets. It's taken me months to get this information so don't let nothing go wrong. Ernie and you create the distraction at exactly one minute to two and me and the boys will get in there, grab it and get out. Whatever you do don't lose this note! Memorize it and destroy it. If you mess up you know what the score will be! Signed, Mr Big

Divide the class into three groups and get them to act this out and continue it. Remind the students to act this all the way through from the beginning. Suggest to them a few ideas about what might happen next. Here are some ideas to help them:

○ They could discuss if the note is real or a joke.
○ They could discuss the possibility of just keeping the money and saying nothing to anyone.
○ They may decide to tell the police. One student could be a police officer on duty at the fair and they call him over and show him the note. This could lead to other police officers lying in wait to catch the crooks red-handed.
○ Perhaps they notice a shady-looking character following them. They become scared. Is that Ed, the one who lost the wallet and is now looking for it? They may decide for that character to confront them and threaten them.
○ Should they find Mr O'Reilly and tell him?

Once a few ideas have been hammered out, run the play through again and continue it using those ideas. Try out different alternatives and get the class to reflect on which version was best, and why.

THE FORMAL INTERVIEW

AIM: To act out formal interviews.

There are many reasons why a formal interview might take place:

o   an interview for a job
o   a disciplinary
o   a complaint
o   a request for a loan at a bank
o   a police interview.

An interview is not like ordinary conversation because laid-down rules and procedures are followed. Here is an example of a 'competency' interview for an employee who works in a high-street bank. Present are:

A: the manager
B: the employee
C: the union representative

A: "Hallo, how are you?" (introductions, shaking of hands) "Please, sit down."
B: "Very well, thank you."
A: "Now, you've had the letter, you know what this hearing is about?"
B: "Yes."
A: "If I could just read the competency accusation to you: 'The standard time for serving a customer is four minutes and you are taking 15 minutes. Despite warnings, this is falling short of minimum expected standards.' Have you got anything to say?"
C: "Yes. I would like to read, on behalf of my client, a letter received from a customer addressed to the bank, only last week: 'To the Manager, I would like to congratulate your employee, Mr _____, for being so polite and taking so much time with me. I'm old and get confused and hate being rushed. I've told my friends what a great service you get at your bank. Yours sincerely, a very rich customer.'"

A: "Yes, I've read that letter, but this hearing is not about that, it's about speed of service."

C: "But you can't separate these things out. My client provides a great service and attracts new customers. He must not be accused of incompetence . . ." (and so on)

Using the above as a model, ask the students to work out in pairs or small groups different types of formal interviews. Keep the language serious and the tone formal. It helps if the teacher can be the interviewer.

THE MAGIC PEN

AIM: To enjoy an activity that is fun.

A student has been annoying the teacher by using an
unsuitable pen during the lesson. The teacher has
requested to see the student at the end of the lesson
when the other students have gone.

Teacher: "I've told you Barry, it's a normal pen or
nothing! I'm not having you write with this old
thing!"

Barry: "But sir! That pen was given to me by my
grandad. It's a magic pen and I must have it back!"

Teacher: "Don't be so stupid boy! There's no such thing
as a magic pen! As you're being stupid I'm going to
keep this pen until the end of term. You keep getting
it out in lessons despite what I've said, so tough luck!
Now off you go!"

Barry: "I tell you what sir! Let me prove to you it is
magic. Here and now!"

Teacher: "Stop wasting my time Barry, I'm busy today!"

Barry: "But sir, one minute and I'll prove it to you!"

Teacher (looks at him and is not sure, pauses): "Right!
You've got one minute."

Barry: "I will write down what you are thinking with this
magic pen. Now think about something, anything,
and I'll write it down." (the teacher concentrates for a
short while)

Teacher: "OK, go on then . . ." (Barry starts writing
something down; he reads it to himself . . .)

Barry: "You won't like it sir . . ."

Teacher: "Go on then, read it . . ."

Barry (reads what he has written): "I'm fed up with this
job. I'm too stressed. I must phone about my early
pension . . ."

Teacher (looks absolutely amazed): "Let me see that."
(grabs it and reads)

The students may wish to improvise other scenarios
using the magic 'mind-reading' pen or develop some
scenarios that involve other sorts of magic.

TIP: Keep the action rooted in an ordinary, down-to-earth situation and have one person sceptical about the magic. When the magic is shown, find a way to dramatically highlight how amazing it is and, most importantly, make sure the other actor(s) show great amazement in their reactions.

THE ONE WORD, ONE PERSON PLAY

AIM: To explore creatively and dramatically the possibilities that one key word can evoke.

Write a set of words on the board that represent values and themes. Suitable words could be:

○ luck
○ hardship
○ friends
○ love
○ work
○ money
○ courage
○ time
○ honesty
○ honour
○ loyalty
○ trust
○ sport
○ travel.

Ask the students to choose one word and then act out a short one-person play centring on their chosen key word.

The students could describe an example of when that word was especially important in their lives. For example, if the word 'persistence' was chosen, the student could say:

"I think this word and what it represents is very important. My grandfather taught me the importance of persistence. When he was a prisoner of war he used to file away with a metal comb at the iron bars, quietly and slowly and persistently, sometimes for weeks," (shows filing action with hand) "until finally he cut through. He escaped" (mimes climbing out of a window) "and came to this country, married my grandmother" (puts arms around an imagined lover) "who had my mother" (points somewhere and pauses) "who had me." (points to herself) "You see, without persistence I wouldn't be here, would I?" (arms open, huge smile!)

TIP: It is a good idea to allow the students to spend some time jotting down a spider diagram once they have chosen their word. The teacher can then wander around and suggest connections. If the teacher has time, it is useful to have prepared a few examples in the above styles which the students could use, develop and continue.

AIM: To create a dramatic sense of mystery.

SCENE: A DENTIST'S WAITING ROOM

Characters A, B and C are patients sitting, reading magazines, and waiting to be called. D is the receptionist who calls the patients and E is a mysterious person, sitting and staring straight ahead.

The patients are sitting waiting. The receptionist comes out and calls the next patient:

D: "Miss Wilkinson please!" (Miss Wilkinson gets up, perhaps a little nervously, and goes off stage. A few moments pass.)

D: "Mr Brown please!" (Mr Brown rises and goes quite boldly with his chest puffed up bravely.)

D: "Reverend Smith please!" (He takes a deep breath and smiles and walks off stage. A few moments pass and the stranger sits staring into space. The receptionist comes out and looks at her appointments book.)

D: "Excuse me, sir, do you have an appointment?"

E: "An appointment? For what?"

D: "Well this is a dentist's surgery sir."

E: "No. I have no appointment."

D: "Well, if I may ask, why are you here?"

The students have to improvise and work out reasons as to why he is there. Try to add as much mystery as possible. Groups of four can experiment with this and then show each other their results.

To follow up, the students could then work out their own scenarios that involve a stranger and a mystery as to why he is there. They then act it out in small groups and perform to each other.

AIM: For students to imagine that they are from the past and have had a vision of the future through time travel. They explain to their contemporaries the amazing things they've seen using their voices, their gestures and facial expressions.

Imagine that it is the year 1070 in England. Establish a scene in, say, a castle. Perhaps there is a raging fire and a banquet going with minstrels and jesters. Norman soldiers are exchanging war stories. Servants are roasting a pig, and so on.

Ask a small group of students to re-create the feel of a Norman castle. A couple of props can establish a minimalist feel. For example, a couple of simple banners and some early medieval lute music work wonders.

Then something extraordinary happens. A jester explains to one of the soldiers that he can take him on a 'time journey' with a special magic spell he has created. It will only last one minute but it will show him the future. The jester sends the Norman into our present.

Have a student act out the amazement of what he sees in today's world.

After one minute he returns to the castle and tells the people in amazement what he has seen. They naturally assume he has drunk too much wine or has dreamed it up.

The focus of the play is the Norman explaining what he has seen. For example:

> "I swear the truth to you . . . I saw a huge silver fish flying with tremendous unearthly noise! . . ." (a plane)
> "I saw man's image through a clear silent veil . . ." (a window) "One woman spoke to herself, as if possessed of a spirit . . ." (using a mobile phone)

Get the students to explore and develop ways in which everyday things today would seem so incredibly mysterious to the people of the past.

Once they have worked out a few ideas, ask them to act out a small play to show this all happening.

155

THE VANISHED NAN

AIM: To act out a mini-play that involves mystery and a ghostly atmosphere and to imaginatively continue it.

Read the following background story to the students and explain that they are to act out scenes from the story and then continue acting out what might happen next.

THE STORY

Sarah used, as a child, to go to New Hilton in the beautiful countryside and stay with her nan. She acquired a love of railway stations in those days. Tragically, 15 years ago her nan mysteriously went missing without a trace. Although Sarah is 25 and lives hundreds of miles away, every summer she travels with her boyfriend, Dom, to New Hilton to try to research and discover what happened to her nan.

One day she is looking through railway books in a New Hilton second-hand bookshop when she pulls out an old volume and starts flicking through the pages. Suddenly she stops and can't believe her eyes. On page 83 is a photo of her nan on New Hilton railway station! It is certainly her nan, she recognizes the coat. She seems to be pointing at something.

Sarah decides to buy the book and go and show it to Dom back at the guest house. She takes it to the old man on the desk and when he sees the book he becomes quite rude and snatches it back and says, "Sorry, this one's not for sale!"

Sarah tries to persuade him to sell it and points out that there is a precious photo of her nan in it. When the man asks her to show him, to her astonishment, the picture on page 83 shows the railway station but her nan is nowhere to be seen.

After they have acted this out, your students may wish to write a script that completes the story. Allow them to discuss this in groups and then they can act out their different scenarios.

AIM: To act like robots in voice and movement.

SETTING THE SCENE

Imagine with your class that 100 years have gone by and a team of archaeologists has discovered a huge, strange, sealed time capsule. Inside is a set of strange robots. When a button is pressed on each, a special power supply activates a screen which displays that these are information robots. The information they hold relates to the year in which you are teaching this topic, e.g. 2009. Each robot will hold information about a different topic.

To act out this scene you'll need approximately:

o Four archaeologists
o Five information robots.

The scene could start off with the date 100 years in the future and the archaeologists opening the door to the huge capsule and reacting to how strange it all is. They discuss the robots and then start pressing the buttons. Here is an example of what could happen if the button is pressed on the robot that brings up the words 'Food We Ate' on the screen. The android has come to life with strange robotic movements and it says, in a strange robotic voice:

> "Hallo to people of the future. We have been specially manufactured to explain what life was like in the year 2009. I can tell you about the food we ate. It was widely believed that eating five portions of fruit and vegetables per day was good for your health. A lot of people ate *McDonald's* fast food. Do you still have *McDonald's*? I will explain what they produced . . ."

Different robots could report on different things. For example:

o the homes we lived in
o the clothes we wore
o the leisure activities we did
o what transport was like

157

- what technology was like
- what communications were like.

The archaeologists can stop the robots talking by pressing a stop button. They could then discuss what the robot told them, highlighting things they find amazing.

AIM: To explore how relationships can change due to circumstances.

These are the main characters:

○ Mr Bull, aged 50, the rich, smug pier owner; a bully, always angry and shouting; a powerfully built man.
○ Trisha, aged 20, his beautiful daughter who works in the Sea Aquarium on the pier.
○ Andy, aged 22, the pier lifeguard; always posing; boyfriend of Trisha.
○ Douglas, aged 47, runs a kiosk on the pier selling postcards and sweets etc.; run-down sort of man, always having bad luck; no confidence.

Mr Bull has been giving nasty final warnings to Douglas that he either tidies up his kiosk or he is out!

There is a mid-season party and all the pier workers are invited. It takes place in a building at the end of the pier and also outside on the pier (it's a warm evening but the sea is high and very choppy). The drinks are flowing and music is playing.

Prizes are given, with applause and laughter, to various employees and a particularly extravagant prize is given to Trisha and Andy but nothing for Douglas.

Trisha and some other employees are fooling about by the railing at the edge of the pier when the railing gives way and Trisha falls in the sea. Everyone screams for the lifeguard Andy, but the sea is raging and he's too scared to jump in and save her. Unexpectedly Douglas jumps in and drags her to safety. Unfortunately Douglas is badly injured in the rescue.

The scene is set in which Trisha, Andy and Mr Bull are visiting Douglas who is recovering in hospital.

Get your students to discuss in groups how they think relationships between the characters will change, and then act out this scene.

TROUBLE ON THE PIER